The Bowler's Manual

The Bowler's Manual

Third Edition

LOU BELLISIMO

Prentice-Hall, Inc., Englewood Cliffs, New Jersey

Library of Congress Cataloging in Publication Data

BELLISIMO, LOU
   The bowler's manual.

   1. Bowling.   I. Title.
GV903.B4 1974   794.6   74-11170
ISBN   0-13-080473-8
ISBN   0-13-080432-0 (pbk.)

Prentice-Hall International, Inc., *London*
Prentice-Hall of Australia, Pty. Ltd., *Sydney*
Prentice-Hall of Canada, Ltd., *Toronto*
Prentice-Hall of India Private Limited, *New Delhi*
Prentice-Hall of Japan, Inc., *Tokyo*

Contents

Preface

This book tells you not just how it should be done, but how to do it. If you want to learn to bowl, this manual explains the basic techniques. If you are an experienced bowler, you will find many valuable tips about why you are having trouble and how to make the necessary corrections. This third edition pays even more attention to common faults and the three methods bowlers can use to correct them.

Over half the pictures in this edition are new. Like those in the former editions, they were not posed. They show actual errors and corrections as they occurred.

I want to express my appreciation and gratitude to Jim Ekstrom and Jack Anderson for their constructive advice and untiring cooperation. Acknowledgment and thanks are also due Bruce Koppe, Art Baumohl, A. L. Ellingson, Robert D. Clark, and Jeanine Bennett.

My sincere thanks to those bowlers who allowed me to criticize their unorthodox styles and habits to illustrate my points, to the boys on the University of Oregon varsity team who so kindly consented to assist with pictures and illustrations of their styles and who spent many hours with me on this project, both on the lanes and as stagehands and propmen during the taking of photographs.

For the excellent photography, my special thanks go to Jim Hosmer of Eugene, Oregon.

I

First Lessons
in
Fundamentals

1. ORIENTATION

If you can take three, four, or five steps in a straight line while swinging a bowling ball in an easy pendulum, you can master the game of bowling. To be sure, this is an oversimplification; but the student who time after time can coordinate these two movements—steps and arm swing—has the game eighty percent mastered.

The coordination of these two simple movements is called *timing*. Timing is the simple coordination of the arm swing and the feet. It sounds simple, but it is unquestionably the beginning bowler's largest problem, and on occasion it frustrates even the pros. Good timing allows the bowler to place the ball out beyond the foul line naturally without forcing the swing.

Coordination will be easier for you if you keep in mind at all times to *adjust the steps to fit the swing*, not the swing to fit the steps. Develop a smooth pendulum swing, then fit the necessary number of steps to it.

This manual explains the theory behind each principle, and each section includes tips for self-help in mastering a new idea or in correcting a fault. Individualized instruction is stressed, and each student is encouraged to develop his own style at his own pace. Every bowler's style is personal and depends on many variables of general body build, strength, timing, and so on; but each bowler should develop his style within the framework of the proven principles of approach and delivery.

This first chapter is an orientation lesson which will familiarize you with many aspects of bowling. It presents basic information on selection of the proper ball, mechanics of the approach and delivery, methods of aiming, and other topics that you need to know a little about before you can get started. Scoring the game is explained in section 13, which can be read in your spare time.

Finding a Ball That Fits

One of the many reasons for the popularity of bowling is that no special equipment is necessary for the novice, since bowling establishments furnish bowling balls free, and shoes are rented for a nominal charge.

One of your first problems will be to find a ball of proper weight that fits your hand. Use as heavy a ball as you can handle—that is, as heavy a ball as you can deliver without undue effort. An easy test for proper ball weight is to take a trial swing with the ball. If you can control the ball during the trial swing, you can use it for your regular delivery (The trial swing is a complete practice swing *without* releasing the ball; see figure 9.) This test is especially useful to bowlers who do not have the strength to control a heavier ball. You will generally find that "house" balls are numbered so that their weight can be identified by the number series. For example, balls numbered from 1 to 20 may weigh from 10 to 11 pounds, those numbered from 21 to 30 from 11 to 14 pounds. The American Bowling Congress approves weights from 10 to 16 pounds. The Women's International Bowling Congress allows a maximum of 16 pounds but specifies no minimum ball weight.

Fully as important as the weight of the ball is the *span*. The span is the distance from the inside edge of the thumb hole to the inside edge of the finger holes. To find a ball with the proper span for you, insert your thumb all the way into the ball; then stretch your fingers out over the finger holes. A correct fit must have the center of the second joint one-quarter inch past the inside edge of the finger holes, as illustrated in figure 1.

1. The span

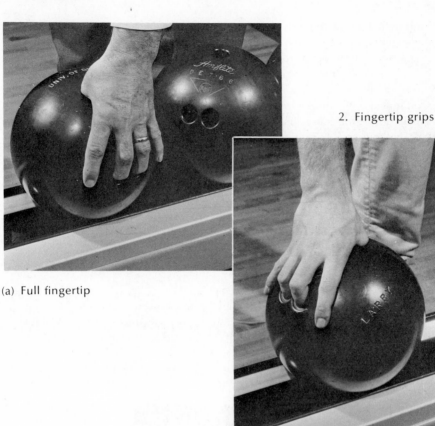

2. Fingertip grips

(a) Full fingertip

(b) Semi-fingertip

A grip where the fingers are inserted to the second joint is a *conventional grip*. This is the recommended grip and should be used by all beginning bowlers. House balls usually have been drilled in this manner. You should be aware, however, that other types of grips are also used. The two most common are the *full fingertip*, figure 2a, and the *semi-fingertip*, figure 2b. These grips are not usually recommended (never for beginners), but bowlers who own their own equipment may employ one of them. The fingertip and semi-fingertip grips are designed to allow the bowler to apply more hook lift with the fingers at the instant of releasing the ball. As the illustrations show, the span is increased with these grips, which allow the fingers to get a longer and more sustained pull or lift on the finger holes. This in turn puts more spin on the ball and consequently more hook. The proper delivery of this type of ball is delicate at best, and the additional hook presents added problems of accuracy.

If your ball fits properly, the span for the ring finger will be approximately one-eighth inch longer than the span for the middle finger. Looking at your hand it appears that the opposite should be true, but by inserting your thumb in the ball you can see how the ring finger moves farther away from the thumb. It is therefore obvious that if a left-hander uses a ball drilled for a right-hander, the span in one of the fingers will be off by about one-quarter inch. The thumb hole should not be too loose, but you should be able to turn the thumb in the thumb hole without much friction. The finger holes should be sufficiently snug to provide a firm grip.

It is impossible for any establishment to stock enough balls to fit everyone. Do the best you can in selecting a house ball, considering weight, span, thumb hole size, and finger hole size, in that order. You should purchase your personal bowling equipment as soon as possible. You are then sure of proper fit, and equipment is available when you want it.

How to Pick Up a Bowling Ball

All bowlers, especially children, should learn the proper way to pick up a bowling ball. For safety, pick up the ball with both hands on the "side" of the ball, as illustrated in figure 3, to prevent your fingers from getting caught between two bowling balls.

3. Picking up the ball

The Stance

The position in which you hold the ball and your body at the start of the approach is the *stance*, figure 4. Different bowlers adopt different stances—some hold the ball chest-high, others chin-high or waist-high, and some will even stoop over with the ball at knee height. Select any stance of those illustrated in figure 5 so long as you are relaxed and comfortable. Keep both hands under the ball and both elbows in close to your sides. Both feet should be reasonably close together, although one foot may be ahead of the other.

The stance position will also vary depending on the number of steps taken in the approach. The bowler in figure 4a takes four steps, therefore his *right* foot

4. Common stances

5. Other common stances

is the starting or push-off step. His weight is mostly on the left foot. The right foot is relaxed. The bowler in figure 4b takes three steps, so she starts with the *left* foot. Figure 4c shows the starting position for the bowler who takes five steps. He uses the low stance position that is popular with many of today's champions.

Chin-High Stance for Women.   The chin-high (or at least chest-high) stance is recommended for women. Rolling the ball fast enough is a problem for most women. The higher ball position in the chin-high stance will make a longer pendulum and generate more speed without extra effort. Most women need this additional speed, but it must be natural, not forced.

Some bowlers should not use the chin-high stance. If you cannot control the swing of the lightest available ball from the higher stance position, then use one of the lower stances. Figure 6 shows the ball pulling the shoulder down as the bowler takes her trial swing.

Figure 7 shows a perfectly smooth and easy trial swing from the lower stance position, which would be recommended in this case.

6. An improperly high stance

7. A correct waist-high stance

Getting Beginners Started

Although this section is devoted primarily to those beginners who are now ready to work on their approach and delivery, any bowler may find this section interesting and helpful in examining his own style regardless of his previous experience.

Bowling is basically a simple game because it consists of two coordinated movements—the swing of the ball and the steps taken in delivering the ball. To be more specific, a bowler develops a smooth, natural swing like the pendulum of a clock, then adds or fits steps to this arm swing. The professionals call this smooth swing *the stroke*.

Since bowling first became popular, instructors have labored to find the easiest method to teach the fundamentals of this smooth stroke. I have experimented with many methods in my twenty-five years of teaching bowling to the beginning student. For both sexes and for any age level, I have found the *three-step approach* perfect for developing sound fundamentals. When a student becomes comfortable with the basics, he may wish to modify his steps as his natural stroke begins to take form. Regardless of the number of steps a bowler wishes to take eventually, the fundamentals demanded by the three-step approach must be mastered first.

The group pictures shown on the following pages are of a beginners' class at the University of Oregon. The last pictures in this section were taken on the ninth class. These beginners need only practice and dedication to become good bowlers. At this point, all of the students could continue using the three-step approach and improve in proportion to their efforts, because they all have good timing, delivery form, and balance. Some students, however, may prefer to change to a four-step approach once they are confident with the three-step approach. The reasons for this change and the very simple method to accomplish it are discussed later in this section.

The beginner should master the instructional techniques in the following sequence:

1. Trial swing
2. One-step delivery
3. Dry run
4. Complete approach and delivery with the ball

The Starting Position.   Figure 8 shows the bowler in the *starting stance position.* Since I recommend the three-step approach for beginners, she is standing approximately 18 inches in front of the 12-foot line of dots. Taller people should start *on* the 12-foot dots.

A set starting position for beginning bowlers is not recommended until their bowling has been evaluated. Move back a bit if you feel you are crowding your approach; move up a little if you are finishing your approach too far behind the foul line. Likewise, the beginner's position to the left or right on the approach is decided by experimentation. For a start, right-handers can straddle the approach board having the second spot in from the right, left-handers the one having the second spot in from the left. This spot is usually on the fifteenth board. Your target from this starting position should be the second arrow in. This is satisfactory in the beginning, since more subtle choice of target is not yet important. You will want to try different starting positions for a few games until you find the most comfortable spot.

8. Starting stance position

9. The trial swing

The Trial Swing. Take a trial swing as shown in figure 9a. Remember that the trial swing is always made without moving the feet and without delivering the ball. From your stance position the ball will go out, down, back, and forward, and then return to the starting position. Have a firm grip on the ball so it won't slip from your hand on the forward swing. Practice the trial swing until the pendulum of the arm is straight and smooth and without any hesitation.

It is important to let the weight of the ball carry it down and its momentum carry it into the backswing. Don't be tempted to force it down and back or be too cautious to let the ball swing freely. Too much caution will result in an attempt to carry the ball back to the backswing. Let the ball swing of its own weight through the downswing into the backswing, and from the top of the backswing forward and up to the starting position. Your instructor may have to assist you as shown in figure 9b.

Figure 10 shows the instructor in a class situation. He checks the students individually as they take a trial swing to be sure that the ball fits properly, that the fingers are in the appropriate holes, and that the ball is the proper weight. If the ball weighs too much, it pulls the shoulders down; a ball that is too light also causes problems. The instructor should check to see whether the swing is too fast or too hard, and whether the student is carrying the ball instead of swinging it like the pendulum of a clock. *Warning*: beginners should not take the trial swing anywhere but on the approach facing the pins, as shown in figure 10. Then if the ball slips out of your hand because it does not fit properly or is too heavy, or because it is swung too hard, it can only go down the lane.

10. Class taking a trial swing

The One-Step Delivery.   You are now ready for your first attempt to roll the ball down the lane. The one-step delivery, which is actually the last sliding step of the complete approach, will help you develop an easy, fluid delivery form. Practicing without the ball makes it easier to take one step and do the important things: bend the front knee, bend slightly at the waist, keep the toes pointed straight ahead. Concentrate on balance, facing straight ahead, and the pendulum swing and follow-through.

For perfect execution of the one-step delivery:

1. Bend the left knee (right knee for a left-hander) as in figure 11c.
2. Lean the body slightly forward (figures 11c and 11d)
3. Follow through all the way up with the arm (figure 11d)
4. Keep the right foot directly behind and in contact with the approach (figures 11c and 11d)

Note that the bowler in figure 11a is in his normal stance position except that he is standing approximately four feet behind the foul line, with his entire weight on the right foot. Taking a set position, he swings the ball all the way back to the top of the backswing (figure 11b). The right foot may move slightly from the weight and motion of the ball, and this movement should be of no concern.

Next, he swings the ball forward easily and smoothly and simultaneously steps forward with the left foot (see figure 11c). Notice the bowler does *not* lift the back foot off the approach; he merely shifts his weight forward to the front foot. Most important, remember not to step too soon or to force the ball as you bring it forward. Bowlers trying the one-step delivery for the first time tend to throw the ball too hard. The arm continues all the way up to the side of the face and stops (see figure 11d). If you can't pose for at least one second in this position, you are not in balance.

Stay with the one-step delivery. Don't be too anxious to move on to the next operation. This is time well spent. In fact, at this point, I suggest you count to yourself—1, 2, 3—or say to yourself—down, back, forward. This will help you develop and feel the smooth, free-swinging pendulum that is vital when you begin taking steps.

11. One-step delivery form

12. One-step delivery   (a) Without the ball
                                         (b) With the ball

    Figures 12 and 13 show an instructor working on the one-step delivery with his class. In figure 12a, he has the entire group in tandem formation on the approach. Notice that they are doing the one step *without* the ball and are under close observation. Figure 12b, the next operation, has one person on each lane taking the one step *with* the ball. This is their first attempt at rolling a ball down the lane. (The unison activity pictured here is definitely not recommended. It was done in this class merely to show that the entire group is doing it correctly). Notice particularly the release and pose. Forcing the pose now means a natural pose and perfect balance later. Often the instructor finds it necessary to assist a pupil with the follow-through as shown in figure 13. The follow-through is one phase of instruction that cannot be over-emphasized with the beginner since many bowlers tend to neglect this fundamental as they become more experienced.

13. Assisting with the follow-through

The Dry Run.   The dry run, or trial run, coordinates the steps with the arm swing, from the starting position to the delivery position, but it is done *without* the ball (see figure 14).

14. The dry run

To begin, shorter persons stand approximately two feet in front of the 12-foot line. Taller persons stand near the 12-foot line, as shown in figure 15a. You will work out the exact distance for your approach steps as you get the feel of the length and speed of your steps.

Take three fast walking steps from the stance position to the foul line. Do not run, poke along, or hesitate. On the third step, bend the left knee just as you did in the one-step delivery. The steps taken are *left, right, left,* and the arm swing is *down, back, forward.* You are doing it correctly when you are able to finish at the foul line and pose as the class in figure 15b.

15. Class practicing the dry run

16. Instructor assisting in the dry run

Your steps and arm swing must be smooth and without hesitation. Most beginners have a tendency to run up to the foul line which results in complete loss of balance. Simply repeat the dry run until you slow down enough to maintain balance and pose. Your instructor may be able to help you by taking your right hand in his left and going to the foul line with you (see figure 16). As soon as you have coordinated this smooth pendulum swing with the three fast walking steps, you are ready to try it with the ball. This motion can be practiced at home using a steam iron or similar object that you can hang onto.

The Complete Approach and Delivery. You are now ready to take the full approach and deliver the ball. Did you charge to the foul line as if someone might steal the ball before you got there? Most beginners tend to go too fast. Make your approach easily and smoothly, letting the weight of the ball do the work of swinging. Don't "muscle" the ball downwards at the start of the forward swing as the last step is taken.

Take the full approach and delivery several times so the instructor can see that your coordination and timing are satisfactory. He will watch for major faults that should be corrected immediately. Normally on your first few tries he will look only for an understanding of the basic approach and delivery.

17. Good delivery form

You will likely roll some of your first few attempts into the left channel. Novices generally pull the arm across in front of the body as they release the ball. This is called *pointing* the ball. Do not be too concerned with the direction of the ball at this time. Accuracy will come after mastery of the proper footwork and timing, after the development of a smooth, fluid arm swing and coordinated footwork. A great improvement can often be made by following through with your arm swing straight out in a line to the second arrow. The coordination of arm and foot movement in a smooth approach and the essentials of an acceptable delivery position should be uppermost in your mind.

Figure 17 shows the fine delivery form displayed by a class taught using the three-step method. All students show perfect balance, are facing straight ahead, and were able to release the ball and pose for the photo of the follow-through— in spite of the distraction of bowling simultaneously for the camera. A person learning to bowl on his own would go through the same procedure step by step.

The key to the proper coordination of the feet and the arm swing (timing) in the three-step approach is bringing the ball down instantly with the taking of the first step. The ball *must* be at the bottom of the downswing at the completion of the first step, as shown in figure 18.

Your instructor will want to watch you briefly so that he can know what phase of your game most needs attention. Proper approach, timing, and coordination are the first concerns; proper delivery form is a secondary objective. Your teacher will point out to each student the faults to which he should pay special attention. The faults may be forcing the forward swing, losing balance during the delivery, twisting the arm during the pendulum swing, a crooked approach, or a poor rolling ball. When your instructor mentions a particular fault, refer to this manual

18. First step ball position

for detailed instructions on how to correct the fault. Do not attempt self-help in any phase of your game, such as developing the hook ball or changing from three to four steps, unless your instructor recommends it. Separate sections are devoted to these subjects at the appropriate time.

The instructor cannot work with everyone at the same time. When he is working with another student, don't waste your time in halfhearted attempts. You are only expected to develop approach, timing, and coordination at this point; if you are having trouble, review these topics in section 1 so that you can get a mental picture of what you are trying to accomplish.

Your instructor may want to change your starting position in order to help your accuracy, even though accuracy is of secondary importance at this time. If you develop a natural hook, for example, your ball will miss the pins by going by them on the left, although you have hit your target spot squarely. In this case you should move your starting position to the left a bit (see section 6). Or if you roll a straight ball, you may find that straddling the fifteenth board and hitting the second arrow will not hit the head pin; then move your starting position to the right.

One special bit of advice: some students, especially men, tend to throw the ball instead of rolling it. Do not force the forward swing for extra speed. Let the ball come through the forward swing naturally. Remember: roll the ball, don't throw it.

Changing from the Three-Step to the Four-Step Approach

You should now have a fairly good stroke for a beginner. You should be facing straight ahead and have good balance and a straight pendulum swing. The proper hand position will be discussed later.

Is a change from three steps to four steps really necessary? For years, the three-step approach, although used by some great bowlers, was frowned upon. In order to be considered a top performer, a good bowler simply had to employ a four- or five-step approach. Unfortunately, we have no statistics to defend a position on the number of steps in the best approach, and thus the entire matter becomes an issue of individual preference. The main goal is to *keep the pendulum swing smooth*. I will leave it to you and your instructor to decide on the change. However, women who need added ball speed should make the change to the four-step approach at this point. The average woman bowler needs the extra ball speed guaranteed by the higher stance and push-away of the four-step approach.

The change from a three-step to a four-step approach is quite simple. Take your usual starting position; then move *straight back* on the runway about 18 inches to make room for the extra step. Now take your regular approach, but (1) carry the ball one full step before you start the downswing; and (2) start with your *right* foot, not your left, as you have been doing. You may find yourself making these changes correctly on the first try, since you will make *no change* in your arm swing rhythm. The only changes are carrying the ball through the first step and taking the additional step, starting with the right foot.

As you practice this simple routine, you will develop the push-away unconsciously and will start the ball moving with the first step. This is exactly what you want to do—coordinate the push-away with the first step, as illustrated in figure 19.

The push-away will usually become automatic after a few games. If you have difficulty in remembering to start with the *right* foot, raise your right heel off the runway and shift your weight to your left foot in the stance position. This will remind you to step off on your right foot.

19. Changing from a three- to a four-step approach

20. Four-step approach   (a) Stance

(b) Push-away

Figure 20 shows the class making the change from the three-step to the four-step approach. Notice that the girl illustrated in figure 19, as well as the entire class in figure 20b, automatically push the ball out in front of the body on the first step, even though they are told to carry it. This push-away is, of course, what should be done, but the concept of carrying the ball lets each beginner develop the push-away instinctively, rather than having to think "step and push" while he is learning.

Figures 20c and 20d show the fine finished product. Without question, learning to bowl using this method practically ensures a good stroke and good delivery form. In some cases, the beginner will bring the ball *down* too soon in the push-away instead of out in front only. In this case, the instructor can assist by steering the arm forward, as shown in figure 21.

(c) Release

(d) Pose

21. Assisting the push-away

2. THE MECHANICS OF BOWLING

The Four-Step Approach

Students will now have some idea of how to approach the foul line and deliver the ball, either by some prior experience or by a degree of mastery of the basic principles outlined in the previous section. The rest of this manual will cover the finer points of the game, yet the skills of a coordinated approach and delivery are fundamental to learning and applying those points. Therefore, all bowlers, regardless of present experience or proficiency, should have a working knowledge of the instructional methods introduced in the previous section and developed more fully in this section. These simple methods serve not only to get the novice

22. The coordination of the swing and the four-step approach

(a) Stance

(b) Push-away

(c) Downswing

started properly, but also to point out and to correct flaws that develop at any stage.

As mentioned in the previous section, there is no reason why a bowler must change from a well-coordinated three-step approach and delivery, although nearly all of today's champions use a four- or five-step approach. Five steps are not generally recommended, especially for the beginner, but your instructor can judge best the proper number of steps to achieve a smooth and consistent approach and delivery. The four-step approach is by far the most popular, and nearly all bowlers can master it. Figure 22 shows the proper coordination of the arm swing and the steps.

(d) Backswing

(e) Forward swing

(f) Delivery and follow-through

When you take your stance position (figure 22a), take a firm, comfortable grip on the ball, with both hands under it. Hold the ball slightly to the right of the center of the body; let the left hand do most of the work of supporting the ball. The positions of the index and little fingers have little to do with the grip. They may be close in or spread out, whichever is comfortable. The feet should be together, and the elbows should be close to your sides.

Push-Away.   The push-away (figure 22b) is the take-off in the approach. Just before you start the push-away, shift your weight to your left foot (the foot that stays in place when you step off with the other foot), so that the first step can be taken with the right foot, smoothly and without lurching forward. With the start of the first step, start the ball forward and push it out to the *full arm's length* with the first step. Be careful, however, not to push the ball out too far, which would cause too long a first step and possibly a delay in the arm swing. These two movements—push-away and first step—must be made together for a good four-step approach.

Second Step.   On the second step of the approach, the ball moves from the end of the *push-away* to the bottom of the arc of the downswing. The left foot completes the second step at the same time that the ball reaches the bottom of the arc (figure 22c).

Third Step.   As the third step is completed, the ball should reach the top of the backswing, approximately shoulder-high (figure 22d). The right shoulder is the pivot point for the pendulum, and the pendulum swing must be in a straight line over the ball's intended path. The line of your shoulders should be at right angles to the ball's path. There is no prescribed position for the left arm during the approach. Use it naturally for balance.

Fourth Step.   On the fourth step, the slide step, the ball and the left foot will start forward at the same time if your timing has been good (figure 22e). If your timing is not correct, the left foot (slide foot) will get to the foul line before the ball is in position to be delivered out onto the lane. When you get "out of time" this way, you will force the speed of the forward swing in an effort to "catch up." This will generally cause the ball to drop in back of the foul line. The black marks you see on the approach in back of the foul line are made when the ball is dropped in this way.

The most overworked phrases in bowling—"Pitch the ball out"; "You're dropping the ball"; and "You're forcing the ball"—all imply the same thing: the approach is not properly coordinated and the slide foot is consequently arriving at the foul line before the ball. Incidentally, the length of the slide is immaterial. It will vary depending on the approach speed, the bowler's height and weight, etc. The bowler illustrated has a long, smooth slide as shown in figure 22e. Although many bowlers depend on the slide to bring the body to a smooth stop, some bowlers have no perceptible slide at all. Their style enables them to maintain balance during the delivery without one. Proper balance during the delivery is the important consideration, not the length of the slide.

Walking Straight. To develop accuracy and form, take your steps to the foul line along a straight line. Check the position of your left foot at the foul line after you have delivered the ball. Did you drift to the right or left of your starting position? It will be too late to correct the delivery just made, but if you check for drifting to either side you can work to avoid repeating errors. Develop the habit of occasionally noting your finishing position at the foul line.

Delivery Form

The position of the body at the foul line as the ball is delivered is called the *delivery*. Delivery form is divided into three distinct parts: (1) facing straight ahead, (2) balance as the ball is released, and (3) straight pendulum swing and follow-through. Individual styles vary because of differences of height, build, strength, speed of approach, etc., but these three elements are fundamental to delivery form.

Facing Straight Ahead. With your shoulders level and parallel to the foul line, you will face straight ahead more easily if you bend your left knee and shift your weight to your left leg. The slide foot should, of course, point straight down the lane during the delivery. Some bowlers find that keeping the right foot on the approach, as shown in figure 23, will help guide the body to face straight ahead. Many bowlers, however, have to throw the right leg around to the left for balance. It is not essential to keep the right foot on the approach. The important thing is to keep the shoulders perpendicular to the line of flight of the ball, that is, parallel to the foul line. However, we recommend that beginners make every attempt to keep the right foot directly behind and on the approach (figure 23).

23. Right foot as a guide

24. Squaring the shoulders with the foul line

The bowler in figure 24 bends forward, very low, and is waving his right leg in the air. The important thing is this: he is facing square with the foul line. Therefore this is an acceptable delivery, because it is natural for him to bend in this manner as he delivers the ball.

Balance.   Try to deliver the ball in perfect balance, as if you were posing for a picture like figure 25.

25. Perfect balance

Straight Pendulum Swing and Follow-Through. (figure 26) The motion of your arm during the approach is a smooth pendulum swing—out, down, back, forward, and follow-through. From the end of the push-away, gravity pulls the ball down and inertia moves it into the backswing. It is not necessary to strain to reach the top of the backswing. Gravity and inertia again bring the ball down and forward to the point of release *without forcing*. Guard against variations in your pendulum swing. Beginning bowlers tend to bring the ball around behind the body during the backswing instead of straight back. Any variation from a perfectly straight pendulum swing increases the chance of missing your target.

26. Straight swing and follow-through

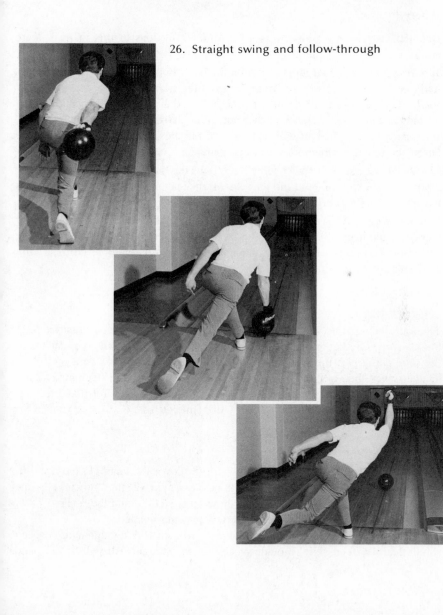

Many champion bowlers have unorthodox styles. They realize their faults better than anyone else does, but through constant practice they have integrated their faults into their style so successfully that they can deliver the ball the same way. every time. *Consistency* is the answer to better bowling. It is far easier, however, to develop and maintain consistency with an easy, smooth, graceful approach and a delivery that does not contain a basic flaw. If stars with unorthodox styles were to give you any tips, they would insist that you learn to bowl the easy and comfortable way—the correct way.

Where to Aim

Detailed instruction on aiming is given in later sections of this manual. Here briefly are the three generally accepted methods:

Spot Bowling.   The target is a spot on the lane. For the strike ball, it will generally be the second arrow or (triangle) from the right edge of the lane. A spot bowler does not look at the pins as the ball is delivered. He concentrates on rolling the center of the ball over the spot. If the delivery is consistent each time, and the spot is hit, the ball will strike the pins in the same place each time. Nine out of ten bowling champions use this method.

Pin Bowling.   A pin bowler aims directly at the pins. If you feel you can be more accurate by aiming at the pins, by all means do so. If your accuracy does not improve as you progress, try a different method of aiming.

Line Bowling.   This method is similar to spot bowling except that the bowler picks an imaginary line rather than a target spot over which he tries to roll the ball. Line bowling is used by a number of bowling champions, but it is a bit advanced for the beginning bowler.

The Foul Line

The foul line separates the approach runway from the lane. It is against the rules to touch *anything* beyond the foul line. A foul is usually committed by the toe of the shoe going past the foul line as the ball is delivered. It is also a foul if the hand touches the wall or anything else past the line. In the beginning, don't worry about stepping or sliding over the line; concentrate on form and timing. Learning to stay bʌck of the foul line will come later.

The Ball's Path to the Pins

A bowling ball may take three possible curves down the lane: (1) the right-to-left curve—of which the *hook ball* is the best example; (2) the "no curve"—the *straight ball*; and (3) the left-to-right curve—the *back-up* and the *reverse hook.* (These names are applied to curves thrown by right-handers.)

All men should learn to roll the hook ball; women with enough natural speed should learn it if possible, though mastery of the straight ball will be adequate for them. Do not develop the back-up and reverse hook, because they are ineffective. The *curve*, which you may have heard of, is merely an exaggerated hook.

Bowling Etiquette

Rules of etiquette are as much a part of bowling as knocking down the pins. They are only common sense practices, but we may sometimes forget these little things. Here are some bowling courtesies:

1. Watch the bowlers on your left and right. The first person who is ready to bowl must be allowed the courtesy of delivering his ball first. Two bowlers on adjoining lanes are *never* to start their approaches at the same time. This is an important rule everywhere.
2. Do not pick up your ball when the bowler on the adjoining lane is ready to bowl. If you do, it will interrupt his concentration.
3. Return to the head of the runway when you have delivered the ball. Do not stand at the foul line waiting for the ball to be returned. Remember, the bowler on the adjoining lane is waiting for you to finish your delivery.
4. Always be ready to bowl when it is your turn.
5. Confine your body English to your own lane. It not only distracts bowlers on the adjoining lanes; it could result in an accidental bumping.
6. Do not bring food or drinks into the bowlers' section. A spilled drink could cause an injury or a foul.
7. Remember, splits, misses, and taps are part of the game, so don't get upset when you come up with them.
8. Return your rental bowling shoes to the desk and return the house bowling ball to its proper spot in the storage rack.
9. When you check your coat and hat, also check your temper.

An exception to bowling courtesy has to be made when an instructor and student bowler are working on the runway. The bowlers nearby must try to ignore them.

Three Instructional Methods: The Trial Swing, The Dry Run, The One-Step Delivery

Three important instructional and corrective tools are available to both the novice and experienced bowler: the *trial swing*, the *dry run*, and the *one-step delivery*.

Two things are vital to your understanding of the trial swing: (1) the feet are never moved during the trial swing, and (2) the ball is never rolled.

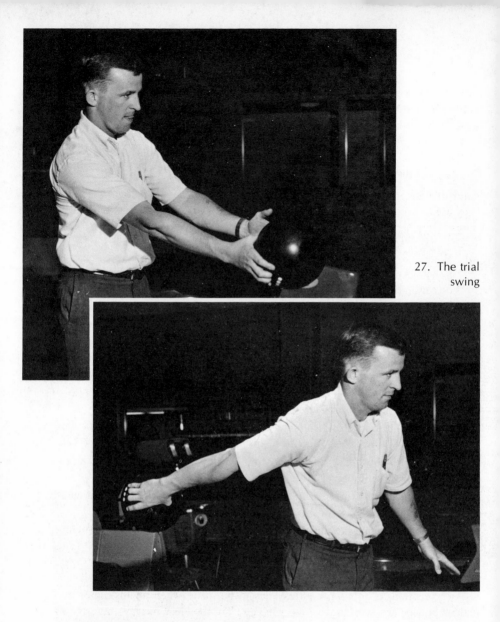

27. The trial
swing

Notice that the bowler's feet are stationary while his arm makes a complete *out*, *down*, *back*, and *forward* motion (see figure 9). This trial swing is basic for beginning instruction and is an invaluable aid in overcoming faults as they develop. Like the approach and delivery, the trial swing is individual. Use whatever stance and ball position is comfortable for you—chest-high, waist-high, or stoop-over stance. Just push the ball out from your regular stance position, swing it down and back, then forward, returning to the starting position, as the bowler in figure 27 is doing. Be sure you understand what is meant by the trial swing, because it is referred to repeatedly throughout this manual.

The *dry run* is illustrated in figure 28. The dry run (or trial run) is simply the complete approach from the stance position to the delivery *without using the ball*. Like the trial swing, it is invaluable for correcting various faults.

28. The dry run

The *one-step delivery* is illustrated in figure 29. This maneuver is in essence the last step of the approach. Like the trial swing and the dry run, it is used in the correction of many faults. To execute the one-step delivery, carry your ball to within four feet or so of the foul line. Take your normal stance position, putting your weight on the foot opposite the sliding foot (a right-hander will have his weight on his right foot, a left-hander on his left foot). Swing the ball down and back into the backswing without moving the feet, then come forward with the ball and the slide foot *at the same time,* as shown in figure 29.

Figure 30 illustrates the one-step delivery *without the ball.* Bowlers often have difficulty getting the hang of the one-step delivery. Doing it first without the ball will make it much easier. Also, practicing this method at home using a steam iron or a similar object will help considerably. Just remember to hold onto the iron! The one-step delivery is explained in detail in section 1.

These methods are appropriate for teaching beginners and for correcting faults, because it is easier to take one step and deliver the ball correctly than it is to take four or five. It is much easier to take the trial swing from a stationary position than it is to swing the ball in the pendulum while taking steps. It is easier to learn and develop good timing and delivery form by making the approach without the ball than it is to learn them with the ball.

29. The one-step delivery

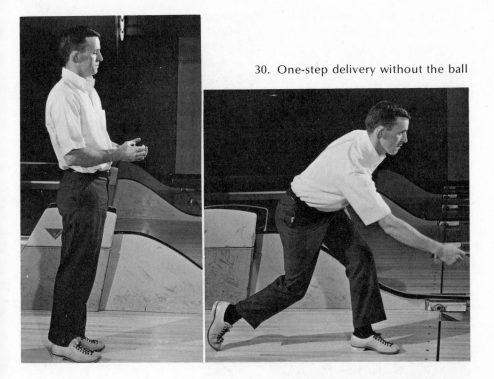

30. One-step delivery without the ball

3. DEVELOPING GOOD DELIVERY FORM

Three Fundamentals

Delivery form and style are affected by many factors—a bowler's size and strength, his natural coordination, the speed of his swing, and the length of his steps. Nevertheless, every student can develop good delivery form by remembering these three fundamentals: (1) face straight ahead as you deliver the ball and as you follow through; (2) be in balance as you complete the slide and delivery at the foul line; and (3) swing your arm in a straight pendulum and follow through directly to your target.

Figure 31 shows four bowlers, each with a different delivery style. Each of these styles is correct, however, because each exhibits the three fundamentals perfectly. Bear in mind that the right shoulder is the pivot point for the pendulum swing and that the arm must be able to swing straight and easily over the intended path of the ball. Turning the shoulders away from parallel to the foul line will hurt your accuracy. These are not the only delivery styles that are acceptable. Observe the three basic rules of a good delivery and develop your own style.

31. Left-handed, right-handed, women, or men:
    The fundamentals are the same

When you practice the fundamentals, "pose" at the foul line after you deliver the ball to develop balance. Forcing yourself to pose at the foul line will eliminate many faults. Try to keep the right foot on the approach directly behind the body during the delivery to help you hold your shoulders parallel to the foul line. As long as you can keep your shoulders parallel to the foul line, you can throw the right leg around to the left for balance if that is more natural for you. The most important single feature of a good delivery is the bent left knee with the left leg supporting almost all the body weight. Your delivery form is good if you can look straight down over your front knee and see your toes pointed straight ahead.

The Follow-through

The follow-through is as important to a bowler as it is to a golfer or a baseball pitcher. A successful bowler must deliver the ball out past the foul line with the arm continuing on through to complete the swing. Don't swing the ball out from the body to the right or to the left across the front of the body. Follow through toward the target, as in figure 32. End your pendulum swing with your hand to the right of your face and you will eliminate the problem of pulling the ball across its intended line of flight. Develop a good follow-through early; it will be a tremendous asset.

If you roll a hook ball, the follow-through encourages the hook lift by the fingers. The straight ahead follow-through will greatly assist the development of

accurate control. The follow-through completes the excellent delivery form of the bowler in figure 32.

Correction of Fouling

Up to this point your instructor has no doubt been overlooking fouls so that you could concentrate on form and timing. If you have been fouling often, the first correction to make is to move your starting position back by the amount that you are going over the foul line plus a six-inch safety factor. If you are starting at the back edge of the approach and you go over the foul line, try shortening your first step. It can be shortened without hurting your timing, but the other steps cannot. If you still foul, your steps are either too long or too fast. To remedy this, count the steps to yourself in a slightly slower tempo as you make your approach.

Correcting the Back-up

The back-up delivery is ineffective and must be avoided. Usually it results from an improperly delivered straight ball. Also, it is more prevalent among beginners who learn to bowl by standing on the left side of the approach and rolling the ball down the middle of the lane, as in figure 33. As the back-up is delivered, the thumb, instead of staying at the 12 o'clock position goes over toward the 1 o'clock position (see figure 33). This causes the fingers to apply a slight left-to-right rotation to the ball, and it fades to the right as it rolls down the lane.

33. Back-up delivery

No star bowler rolls a back-up ball, because this delivery is unproductive no matter how accurately made. To be effective, a ball must drive into the pins after hitting the head pin. The back-up does just the opposite. It deflects off the head pin much more than the straight ball or the hook ball, and it does not drive in to knock down the five pin. Nor does the back-up ball have a consistent line of flight. Varying the position of the thumb between the 12 and 1 o'clock positions causes the ball to go straight one time and to back up more than normally at another time.

You cannot roll the back-up unless you twist your arm and wrist clockwise as you release the ball. Keeping the arm stiff and straight and the thumb at the 10:30 o'clock position will eliminate the back-up. To correct the back-up, stand in your regular stance position holding the ball at your side (see figure 48). Your thumb should be at the 10:30 o'clock position. Thus a line drawn between the middle finger and the ring finger should be around the 4:30 or 5 o'clock position (see figure 34). The hand must be in this position as the ball is delivered in order to eliminate the back-up.

Now take a trial swing. Swing the ball out, down, back, and up again, keeping the arm straight and the thumb at the 10:30 to 11 o'clock position, fingers at the 4:30 to 5 o'clock position. Repeat this swing a few times. When you can keep your arm straight and your hand in the correct position, make your regular

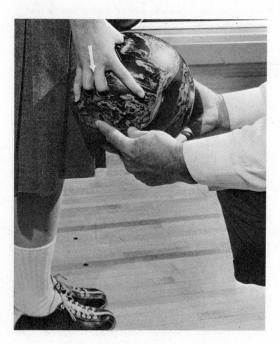

34. Correct hand position

35. Correct
delivery

approach and deliver the ball (see figure 35). If this does not correct the back-up
for you, try some of the following ideas to learn the proper hand position.

The stationary approach remedy illustrated in figure 36 may be helpful. In
this method, two bowlers roll the ball back and forth to get the idea of the proper
hand position. Your instructor will show you how to roll the ball so that there
will be no wild throws and consequent possible injuries. If you don't pick up the
proper hand position in the first few rolls with your instructor, get another student
to go with you to the rear of the settee area, if possible onto a rug, and to roll the
ball back and forth to you until you get the proper hand position. Then try to
make a correct delivery on the lanes.

36. Stationary approach

If these methods don't work for you, try the method of shaking hands with a person standing just beyond the foul line as you deliver the ball (see figure 37). He should stand facing you just at the right-hand channel of your lane. Force your right hand to come through the downswing in the handshake position with the open end of the "V" made by the thumb and index finger facing the pins.

If none of these methods breaks your habit of twisting the arm and wrist during the downswing, try one of these exercises. Stand at the foul line in your delivery position (figure 38) or make a one-step delivery of the ball (figure 29). Roll the ball down the lane. Concentrate on keeping your arm straight and your fingers at the 4:30 to 5 o'clock position. The important thing is not to twist or turn the arm at all. Repeating one of these exercises enough times will probably correct the back-up for you.

Practicing at home swinging an electric iron helps considerably. It is merely a case of getting the feel of the thumb pointed towards the body and the fingers on the "outside" of the ball.

If these cures fail, you should ask your instructor or another qualified person to asist you by holding your wrist firmly in the proper position as you make a one-step delivery (see figure 39).

38. Standing delivery

37. Handshake

39. Holding the wrist firm

4. PLAYING SPARES

The Three Basic Spare Angles

If all ten pins are knocked down by the first roll in a frame, a strike is scored. If the first roll leaves one or more pins standing, the rules allow a second roll, just one chance, to knock down the remaining pins. The pins that remain standing after the first roll are referred to as a *leave*. Knocking down the leave scores a spare; bowlers say that the spare is *converted*.

Good spare shooting is the foundation of top bowling. Should you miss a spare, it will generally take three strikes in a row, a *turkey*, to gain ground on the bowler who is getting good counts and converting his spares.

Three basic aiming angles are used to convert spares. These are center-to-center; left-to-right; and right-to-left. The first, the strike position, is a center-to-center angle (see figure 40a). Leaves of the 4-pin, the 7-pin, or both, are played from right to left (see figures 40b, 40d). Leaves on the right side of the lane, such as the 6-pin or the 10-pin, are played from the left-to-right angle (figure 40c).

To convert the 10-pin, all right-handed bowlers who roll a hook (or curve) ball should aim at the third arrow from the right. If they roll a straight ball (no

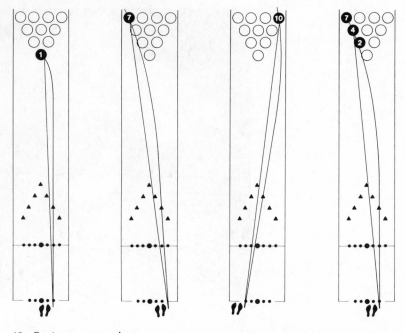

40. Basic spare angles

(a) Center-to-center   (b) Right-to-left   (c) Left-to-right   (d) Right-to-left

hook or curve), they should position their feet on the same board, but aim at the center or fourth arrow (see figure 40c). To convert the 7-pin, they should aim somewhere between the second and third arrows (figure 40b), depending on the amount of hook. (Left-handers count the arows from the left, of course.) Figure 40d shows the conversion of the 2-4-7 pin spare by the right-handed hook and straight ball.

These illustrations show that the ball passes over the second or third arrow or somewhere in between them in all three basic spare angles. Thus the second and third arrows are the only targets a bowler needs. Changing the location of the stance position makes all other necessary adjustments.

The professional bowler who rolls the ball inside (to the left of) the center arrow or outside (to the right of) the first arrow is making an extremely delicate adjustment, seeking the maximum benefit of an angle he feels is best for the lane conditions he faces. Such fine adjustments are matters of individual expert style.

As a rule, a leave that includes the 1- and 5-pins should be converted from the center-to-center angle. All other spares that include the head pin, a few of which are illustrated in figure 41, should be played from the left or right. First assume the strike position, then move the feet a board or two in or out according to what other pins are left with the head pin and the amount of hook on the ball.

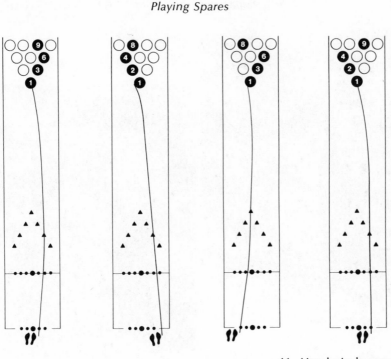

41. Head pin leaves

An exception to this rule is the 1–3–6–8 leave illustrated in figure 41c. This is a common leave for beginners. Increase your chances of converting this difficult spare by playing over the center arrow.

There are so many different combinations of pins that can be left after the first roll that it is impossible to list them all here. That is why we suggest the three basic spare angles as explained in this section.

Figure 42 illustrates the conversion of the 2–4 spare. Imagine the line that will be the intended path of the ball. This line will go from the outside edge of the right shoe to the spot you wish the ball to hit. If you are a spot bowler, move a bit on the approach until this line crosses a convenient target—usually the second or third arrow. This imaginary line is similar to sighting a gun—the rear sight is the spot at the foul line over which you intend to roll the ball, the front sight is the target arrow on the lane. The pin bowler will use the same method, only his target in this case will be the 2-pin. It makes no difference how much hook, if any, the bowler rolls. The above system will work provided the imaginary line the bowler draws corresponds with the exact amount of hook he rolls.

Therefore, straight ball or hook, the principle is the same. You line up your sights, walk in a straight line *parallel with this line*, and roll the ball over this imaginary line and over the target.

42. Converting the 2–4 spare

43. Converting the 5–9 spare

Figure 43 shows the proper method of playing the 5–9 spare. The more left-to-right angle a bowler can play on this spare, the less chance he runs of chopping the front pin off the back pin *(picking a cherry)*. This same principle, of course, also applies to other spares where a chop of the front pin is a distinct possibility, such as the 6–10, 2–5, 3–6, etc.

As a point of information for the novice, if, for example, you are trying to convert a corner pin for a spare and your ball drops into the channel in front of the pin, but the wobble of the ball in the channel hits the pin, it is *not* a spare. Once the ball has left the lane surface, any pins it knocks down *do not* count.

5. ROLLING THE HOOK BALL

All top bowlers roll a hook ball. Why? Because it will get more strikes. Figure 44 shows the ten pin triangle and the ball. The ball is rolled into the 1–3 pocket; then it hits between the 5- and 9-pins so that the 5-pin can take out the 8. This is the normal strike pattern. If the ball is to be effective, contact with the head pin must deflect it as little as possible from this normal path.

Applying a spin to the ball as it is released causes it to curve into the pins. The inertia from the curve offsets the tendency of the ball to deflect after striking the head pin; the ball digs in and drives into the 5-pin. In the normal strike pattern the ball must hit the 5-pin, which is therefore called the king pin. Since the 5-pin is directly behind the head pin, the ball may miss the 5-pin if it deflects after hitting the 1–3 pocket. Remember that the ball is rolling like a wheel, not spinning like a top.

The hook ball gives the bowler a "bigger" pocket; that is, the ball need not always hit the exact center of the 1–3 pocket to be effective, because the right-to-left drive of the ball into the pins affords a much higher probability of hitting the 5-pin. The "high" hits (those closer to the head pin) and the "thin" hits (those closer to the 3-pin) have a better chance of striking with a good hook ball. Figure 45 shows the normal strike pattern. Notice that there are three different pin spreads:

1. Ball hits the head pin, which hits the 2, the 2 hits the 4, and the 4 hits the 7.
2. Ball hits the 3, the 3 hits the 6, and the 6 drives into the 10.
3. Ball hits the 5 and the 9, and the 5 hits the 8.

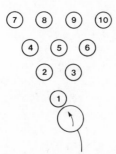

44. Normal strike ball path

45. Normal pattern

46. Hand position for the hook

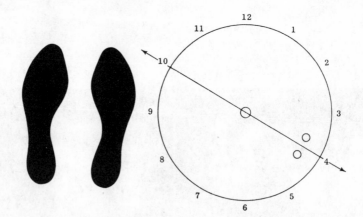

47. Thumb hole at 10 o'clock

48. Beginning routine for the hook

Figure 46 shows an instructor demonstrating the hook ball. Notice the position of the hand at the instant the ball is released. The wrist is rigid, not broken, and the fingers are "closed" to apply the lift straight up for hook spin. As the ball slides off the thumb, the fingers lift counterclockwise to impart the hook spin or lift to the ball.

As you look down on the ball, your thumb position must be between the 10 and 10:30 o'clock positions. This places the fingers between the 4 and 5 o'clock positions (see figure 47). With the thumb hole in the center of the ball, the third joint of the thumb will be pointed towards 10 o'clock.

For the first attempt at rolling the hook, follow this routine. Take your regular stance position, holding the ball at your side (see figure 48). Notice that the wrist is straight and firm, not broken, and the thumb hole is in the center with the thumb pointing to 10 o'clock.

Next, bring the ball up to your regular starting position. Keep the grip firm and the wrist rigid and straight.

Now take a trial swing. This one simple little refresher is usually sufficient, but it is advisable to repeat this self-conscious procedure on your first few tries to roll the hook.

49. Trial swings for the hook

If you have difficulty keeping the thumb pointed to 10 o'clock as you release the ball, take a few trial swings in your one-step delivery position as illustrated in figure 49. Keep your eyes on the thumb and fingers during these trial swings, even though you have to drop your head to watch the ball.

If you cannot keep the arm and fingers in the proper position in the trial swing, you will not do so when you deliver the ball. Repeat the trial swing until you can do it correctly every time. Then take a one-step delivery and release the ball.

Two bowlers can practice other good routines for developing the feel of the hook release. Rolling the ball back and forth as illustrated in figure 46 will help them get the feel of the ball coming off the fingers. Tossing the ball back and forth as shown in figure 50 will assist in developing the split second lift, as well as in keeping the arm and wrist stiff and straight. Students who have been having trouble up to this time will often get the feel of the ball coming off the fingers by doing this exercise.

As soon as you begin to develop a consistent hook, you will have to allow for it by changing your starting location. First move in to the left a board or two to allow for the hook. You will still roll the ball over the second arrow for the strike

50. Split-second lift

delivery, of course. Do not try to roll the hook until your instructor can watch you, because it is common for a bowler at this stage to lose proper timing or delivery form, to start to side-wheel, or to twist the arm, drop the shoulder, or spin the ball like a top. Because the bowler cannot see himself, he does not realize that these things are happening. Your instructor should be present when you first try the hook so that he can spot and correct these errors immediately.

Many times a bowler will not be able to get the ball to hook, even though the hand is in the proper position as the ball is released. This is simply a case of not having developed the split-second lift or the right feel of the ball on the tips of the fingers as it is released. This is no cause for alarm. You will soon get the feel of the release and you will develop the required lift.

Once you begin to use the hook ball, you should roll it for both the first and second shots (strikes and spares). Some beginners prefer to roll the hook for the strike and a straight ball to convert the spare. This practice is not recommended.

Many bowlers, especially beginners trying the hook for the first time, get the hand too far around the side of the ball. They hold the ball with the thumb at 9 o'clock, which brings the "line" between the ring and middle fingers to 3 o'clock. The 9 o'clock thumb position may cause the wrist to "break," thereby bringing the hand on top of the ball as the ball nears the point of release (see figure 51). This hand position results in a weaker hook. The wrist breaks because few bowlers have the strength to keep the wrist straight when the entire weight of the ball is controlled by the wrist alone. By having the thumb at 10 to 11 o'clock (the line at 4 to 5 o'clock) as illustrated in figure 52, the palm and

51. Poor hand positions
for the hook

little finger help considerably in carrying some of the weight, making it much easier to maintain a stiff, straight wrist. The 4:30 finger position results in a better hook and a better rolling ball

To develop the proper feel of the hook lift, stand at the foul line and roll the ball down the lane as shown in figure 52. If possible, practice this exercise without pins. Stand to the right of center, roll the ball over the second arrow, and watch it hook into the left channel. Keep the fingers closed and stroke the arm straight up. You will feel the ball come off the fingers.

52. Thumb hole at 10 o'clock

53. Good hook rollers

Figure 53 shows four bowlers who roll very good hooks. Notice the stiff wrist, the finger position at 4:30, and the thumb sliding out first followed by the "closed" fingers, and the split second lift counterclockwise. Keeping the index and little finger in close to the middle and ring fingers will help you keep the wrist rigid. Bear down on the ball with the index and little finger.

A "turn and lift" hook is illustrated in figure 54. This hook is not recommended for beginners. Notice how this bowler rotates the wrist counterclockwise while lifting with the fingers at the same time, which motions give this hook its name. This type of hook is much harder to control and it requires much more practice to achieve accuracy. The two rows of white tape on the ball show clearly how the ball track (the surface of the ball making contact with the lane) turns because of the wrist turn.

The *curve ball* is merely an exaggerated hook. In fact, any slowly rolled good hook ball will curve in a wide arc. Although the curve ball can be very effective as a strike producer, it is not recommended because it presents too many problems of control. In addition to the difficulty of releasing the curve ball consistently, there is the further problem of the physical construction of the lane bed. Various woods are used in the lane bed. Because the curve ball must cross over more boards on its way to the pins than the faster hook must cross, differences in the cellular structure of the wood, its hardness, irregularities in its surface

54. "Turn and lift" hook

finish, and so on, will affect the intended path of the curve ball more than they will the path of the hook ball. It is simple arithmetic: the fewer boards to cross, the smaller the chance for the lane to affect the intended path of the ball.

Figure 55 shows the left-hander applying the hook lift. The difference is merely that the lift is counterclockwise by the right-hander, clockwise by the left-hander.

55. Left-hander's hook

6. SPOT, PIN, AND LINE BOWLING

The most common methods of aiming are known as spot bowling, pin bowling, and line bowling. Is it better to look and aim at a spot on the lane, or is it better to aim directly at the pins? The answer is not the same for every student. Nine out of ten bowling champions aim at a spot on the lane, but one of every ten champions aims directly at the pins. We prefer spot bowling and recommend that all students adopt this system. The majority of beginners will find spot bowling the easier method to master if they give it a fair trial. It is easier to hit a target sixteen feet away than one sixty feet away. True, a miss of one inch at the target spot can mean a miss of five or six inches at the pins; but it is still easier to hit the nearer target.

The spot bowler aims at a spot on the lane, not at the pins. For the strike ball the second arrow from the right is usually his target. He concentrates on rolling the center of the ball over his spot, and if he delivers the ball consistently and hits his spot, the ball will hit the pins in the same place every time.

Many spot bowlers prefer aiming at the spots that are eight feet in front of the foul line. They find this closer target easier to hit. However, beginners who try this method of aiming should be aware of its shortcomings. It may cause dumping of the ball, instead of lifting it, and cutting the follow-through instead of reaching out and up.

The pin bowler aims directly at the pins. In a sense, this is aiming by instinct. Nevertheless the ball must still follow the line that the delivery pendulum gives it. Drifting—walking to the left in the approach—is more of a problem for the pin bowler than it is for the spot bowler. Pin bowlers who stand right of center on the approach in order to get the maximum angle into the pocket invariably drift to the left. The spot bowler, on the other hand, because his arm swing is on a direct line with his target, is able to walk straighter towards his target.

The line bowler visualizes a line over which he wants the ball to travel. He then picks two or three check points on this line (designated by a "C" in figure 56) and concentrates on rolling the ball over the check points.

You may adopt whichever method you wish. However, no matter how you aim—at a spot or directly at the pins—as a beginner you should still try to roll the ball over the second arrow for a strike.

Generally speaking, you have been straddling the fifteenth board in the stance position, and you have been rolling the ball over the second arrow to hit the strike pocket. The fifteenth board contains the second dot from the right. This stance position is used under normal conditions by most bowlers who have an average hook.

If your ball is hooking too much to hit the strike pocket, move your starting location a board or two in to the left. *You will still aim at the second arrow.* If the lane is fast (see section 13) and the ball is not coming up to the pocket,

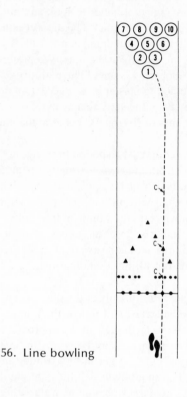

56. Line bowling

the opposite adjustment must be made. Move your starting location out to the right a board or two, but continue to roll the ball over the second arrow.

Many spot bowlers find it difficult to roll the center of the ball exactly over a narrow spot. When they try to put the ball over a certain board or arrow, they stiffen up and lose the proper roll of the ball. In this case *area bowling* is a better method. Instead of trying to pinpoint the ball over a single arrow or board, make your target an area of two or three boards. This method works well not just for beginners; several top bowlers use this system of aiming.

Many experienced bowlers find it easier to pick a different target on the lane than to change their starting position; but this method is usually less successful for beginners. If when the ball rolls over the second arrow it hooks too much, the experienced bowler may aim one or two boards outside of the second arrow. This system has the advantage of keeping the body square with the foul line. You may be one of the rare beginning bowlers who develop a wide, sweeping hook ball in which case you will profit more by changing your target than by moving your starting position far enough to the left to compensate for the wide hook.

II

Common Faults
and
How to Correct Them

When working on correction of specific faults, make sure they are corrected in the order of their overall importance. That is to say, approach-timing problems must be remedied first, then delivery form, then hand position, ball roll, etc. For example, it will be unrewarding to spend time on improving the hook roll when you can't roll the same place twice because of poor delivery form.

Like any other athlete, a bowler can be plagued by numerous problems or faults, some minor, some major. Even a bowler who learned to bowl from a competent instructor and who appears to do everything correctly may suddenly develop a fault.

Sections 7, 8, and 9 of this manual cover the most common faults and explain how you can correct them yourself. However, a qualified person should be in charge when you try the corrections, since most of the methods require him to help you in some way.

If you know what your fault is, check through the following sections to find it discussed. Section 7 deals with problems in the approach, section 8 with the delivery, and section 9 with the roll of the ball.

One word of advice: do not bowl for score when working to correct a fault or to improve your form. Usually your score will suffer during this process, and you should disregard the score temporarily.

Once your approach, delivery, and ball roll are satisfactory, you need only practice to improve your game. Practice will give you the *consistency* that is the secret of better bowling. It is relatively easy to learn to bowl; to master it, like any other sport, requires much practice, patience, and perseverance.

The technique of bowling is made up about 80 percent of approach timing (the coordination of the arm swing and foot movements), 15 percent delivery form (the position of the body at the foul line as the ball is released), and 5 percent of ball roll (the advantages and disadvantages of a particular kind of hook). Thus it is clear that you should consider your approach first, then your delivery position, and finally the ball or hand position.

57. Fitting the steps to the natural swing

7. THE APPROACH

We have already remarked that the two basic movements of bowling, the arm swing and the steps, are simple movements. In presenting the timing of the approach, we described how the four steps—right, left, right, left—"fit" the swing of the ball—out, down, back, forward, and how the three-step approach shows the steps—left, right, left—fitting the swings—down, back, forward.

Now we will examine some of the techniques of timing applied by experienced and professional bowlers. Figure 57 shows the excellent stroke of an experienced bowler. Notice the smooth, free-swinging pendulum. There is no hitch and no forcing at any point in the swing. Notice that the right shoulder, the pivot point of the pendulum swing, remains directly over the intended path of the ball. This bowler's smooth approach shows the importance of *fitting the steps to the natural swing*. The number of steps required is not the important thing. Nor is it critical where the ball is on a particular step. The bowler now must strive for smoother coordination of the arm and feet in order to develop precision. The top bowler wants perfectly consistent timing.

If you do not already have a pendulum swing like this, do a little experimenting. Add a half step or raise or lower your stance position. If you do not already take short steps, try taking shorter ones, which are smoother and more graceful. The important thing is to develop a smooth pendulum swing, and then to fit the steps to your swing.

The Push-away and Timing Problems

The push-away differs for each bowler. Some must keep it fluid and moving, while others actually do better with a slight delay. Some bowlers, women especially, need a higher and longer push-away for added natural speed and for better timing. Good timing depends on a good push-away.

A faulty push-away is one of the main causes of poor approach timing. Many instructors call the push-away "the point of no return," and some feel strongly that a good start assures a good finish. We cannot go this far, but a faulty start can obviously lead to much trouble.

Experiment with the push-away until you find the one that fits you best, the one that gives you the feeling of the best timing and is the most comfortable. Your instructor should be watching when you experiment with the push-away. Some bowlers must put a little more zip in the downswing, others must move the swing a little easier. The important thing is to develop your natural swing. Take trial swings until you can feel the smooth pendulum stroke, then fit the necessary number of steps to this stroke. As for the steps, some are timed for short, fairly fast steps, others who have a slower pendulum swing generally need another step.

Remember: do not alter a good pendulum swing. Instead, fit as many steps to the swing as are necessary.

Correcting a Hop in the Approach

The hop is caused by one of three things: (1) either the arm swing is rushed, so that the arm is at or near the top of the backswing too soon; (2) the bowler's stance location is too close to the foul line and does not leave him enough distance for the full four steps; or (3) the bowler has a natural three-step swing, but he is trying to squeeze in four steps. In this last case, the instructor must watch him and decide what to change.

The hop is generally from the second to the third step in the four-step approach. The left-hander in figure 58 hurries her arm swing.

Notice in figure 58b that the ball should be at the *bottom* of the arc on the second step. Instead the bowler has gone beyond this point and is almost at the top of the backswing. Therefore, with only two steps remaining, she obviously must hurry the third step. The hurrying will cause the hop in this step.

To correct this fault, see that the ball goes no farther than straight out on the first step and no farther than the bottom of the arc on the second step. This leaves time to complete the third step while the ball is going from the bottom of the arc to the top of the backswing. If you are unable to correct this on your own, you may need help from your instructor. Notice in figure 59 that the instructor hangs on to the ball to steer it *out* on the first step, *down* on the second step, not out and down together on the first step. This may take several tries, and often it is also necessary to change the stance position in order to get completely away from the old style.

Standing too close to the foul line is much easier to correct. Simply move the starting position back a foot or so, and take *longer* and *slower* steps. If this does not correct the hop, as it usually does, slide the feet (shuffle) as you approach the foul line. This will always do the job, and as soon as the hop is eliminated, the shuffle will also disappear.

58. Rushing the arm swing

59. Timing the arm swing

Crooked Walk to the Foul Line (Drifting)

A bowler should finish his approach on or near the same board on which he started. There are three deviations from the straight line of walk: some bowlers will angle from right to left on the way to the foul line, others will go from left to right, and others approach in a crooked line. Many champions employ a drift during the approach, but the preferred approach is still the straight line. Those champions who drift in the approach have learned through constant practice to be consistent. This is certainly the harder way, and it is not recommended. Correct the fault of drifting early and you will profit in the long run.

Generally, the bowler who aims directly at the pins (a pin bowler) will have a tendency to drift more than the bowler who aims at the range finders (a spot bowler). Probably nine out of ten bowlers who drift on the approach are pin bowlers. This is often a problem for the bowler who may attempt to take advantage of the outside line to get a better angle and less deflection for his strike delivery. He will often drift to the left and destroy his line, and thus he will miss the pocket.

The crooked approach is so impossible to control that nobody uses it intentionally. To correct a crooked approach, note the boards on which you start and finish. (All bowlers should periodically check where they are finishing, particularly after delivering a bad ball.) Your instructor will have to point out to you on which steps you drift, because you cannot see this yourself. Next mark chalk lines (using an easily erasable chalk) or put down a tape line to indicate where the feet should be, as in figure 60.

Keep your eyes on the tape line as you take your approach, and pay no attention to the target or to your approach direction for the moment. If possible, do this exercise without pins. Often a crooked approach is not easy to correct and will require much time and patience. If the crooked approach is not an effect of another fault (such as rolling a ball that is too heavy, or side-wheeling during the delivery), practice concentrated on eliminating drift is the only solution. You simply will have to slow down and concentrate on *footwork* more than any other phase of the game until a straight walk is developed.

A Hesitation in the Approach

You can get rid of a hesitation in your approach by following the rule, *"fit the steps to the natural arm swing,"* not the arm swing to the steps. Women hesitate more often than men in the approach, generally after the first or third steps of a four-step approach. This hesitation destroys their natural timing and cuts down on the speed of the ball.

To correct the hesitation, go back to the basic instruction for developing the arm swing and the steps. First, take a trial swing and concentrate on a free and easy swing without a hesitation. Next take a dry run and count the steps to your-

60. Tape line guide

self. After three or four dry runs, take your normal approach and deliver the ball. If you are unable to correct the hesitation on your own, have your instructor stand beside you counting to four in the proper tempo to your steps. Repeat the three operations—first, the arm swing without a hesitation, then the steps without hesitation, followed by your normal approach and delivery of the ball. It should not take you long to make this correction with your instructor assisting you

Sometimes the delay or hesitation in the backswing is difficult to correct because the backswing is too high. In this case, refer to the method of correcting the high backswing described in section 8.

Correcting Approach Timing

The importance of approach timing cannot be overemphasized. Nearly every star bowler who has had a bad series in performance will admit that it was because his approach timing was not at its best, that he could not find the "groove."

If you are a beginner and are having trouble with your timing, bear in mind that your steps, assuming you have adopted a four-step approach, are right, left, right, left, in coordination with the pendulum swing of out, down, back, forward. If your pendulum swing is free and easy and without hesitation, say the steps aloud to yourself—"right, left, right, left," or "one, two, three, four"—as you approach the foul line. Remember: the steps must coincide with the pendulum swing in order to have a smooth, rhythmic approach.

If your steps appear to be too fast for the arm swing, experiment with another stance. For example, try a lower stance with more zip in the downswing. Often a bowler will delay at the top of the backswing. For a probable remedy, experiment with a *lower* backswing by holding the ball lower in the stance position.

Many times a beginner will suddenly develop the habit of carrying the ball for two steps without knowing why his timing has gone sour. Remember that the ball goes *out* on the first step, *down* on the second step, and you will usually eliminate the problem of carrying the ball. In most cases if you can get the first two steps properly coordinated, you can forget close attention to the third and fourth steps. They will nearly always be satisfactory, since the ball will have to go up on the third step and down and forward on the fourth.

The beginner's timing problem, unlike the experienced bowler's, is not one of finesse. As a beginner with a four-step approach, don't expect more than a rough out-down-back-forward coordination. The fluid, graceful approach must be developed through practice. You can speed up your development of a smoother, more fluid pendulum swing by taking trial swings and counting aloud the four beats. Counting aloud will help you regulate the speed of the steps to fit your stroke.

The timing problem for the advanced student or experienced bowler is another story. For them the two most common mistakes are taking the steps too quickly and forcing the forward swing. The bowler who charges the foul line can slow down his steps by counting the four beats to himself in the tempo he feels is proper for his natural pendulum swing. If he is forcing the forward swing, the bowler must remind himself to go easy as he starts the ball forward on the last step.

Every bowler should count his steps to himself when he is bowling well so that he will know his individual tempo. Whenever he loses his timing, he can count to himself and spot the error. This is like humming a tune to yourself if you want to dance and there is no music. Count your steps to yourself as you make the approach, and you will learn to recognize the speed-up of a step just as dancers would immediately recognize a change of tempo in music.

Better bowling requires consistency. Consistency of footwork is of vital importance if the tempo of the approach is to be the same each time. The black marks on the runway just back of the foul line are the signs of inconsistent footwork, the result of poor timing. The bowler's feet arrived at the foul line before the arm was in position to deliver the ball. The arm swing was accelerated in an attempt to catch up; but it didn't quite make it and the ball was dropped or forced, familiar terms to most bowlers. Whatever you call it, poor timing of the footwork and arm swing cause the ball to leave the hand before it can be delivered out onto the lane beyond the foul line.

Ahead of the Ball

"Ahead of the ball" is the most overworked phrase in bowling, but it describes a very common problem. To be ahead of the ball simply means that the left foot arrives at the foul line before the ball does. Being ahead of the ball and forcing the forward swing are the two biggest headaches for better bowlers. Figure 61 shows a bowler who was ahead of the ball by a half step, and who forced his swing in order to catch up. As a result, he dropped the ball behind the foul line.

The problem of being ahead of the ball is compounded for the bowler who *turns and dips* at the line, as the beginner in figure 62 is doing. The problem is bad enough when you are facing straight ahead as illustrated in figure 61. When the bowler who turns at the line forces to catch up, it causes him either to pull the ball across in front of the body, or to drop it behind the line.

To correct this fault, first try counting your steps in the tempo you feel is proper for your approach. Take a few dry runs to help slow down your steps. If you cannot make this correction on your own, ask your instructor for assistance as shown in figure 63.

First the instructor will watch you closely as you take a few dry runs to make certain that you are not rushing to the foul line. He will assist you by counting loud in the proper tempo. He will count at the same tempo as you take a trial swing. As soon as you are swinging the ball freely and easily in the proper tempo, he will ask you to take off in the approach, again counting to help you maintain the proper tempo.

61. "Ahead of the ball" by a half step

62. Turning and dipping at the line

63. (a) Dry run to slow down

(b) Trial swing and count

64. Corrected approach

65. Corrected dip and turn

Figure 64 shows the bowler in figure 61 after the correction was made. Notice especially how the ball and the foot arrived at the foul line for the split-second lift and roll at precisely the same moment.

Figure 65 illustrates the beginner after the correction was made. This was done using the same procedure followed in figure 63. This bowler now needs only to work on a better wrist position, and he's on his way.

Being ahead of the ball can also be caused by carrying the ball, that is, not allowing the ball to swing freely in the stroke. Delaying the swing causes the left foot to arrive at the foul line ahead of the arm swing. A correction for carrying the ball is suggested later in this section.

Forcing the Forward Swing

This fault is perhaps the most prevalent of all approach and delivery problems. It bothers both experienced bowlers and beginners. It is the first thing that you should check if you are having trouble with your game.

Forcing the forward swing may be defined as exerting more arm effort than is needed from the top of the backswing to the point of releasing the ball. One of two factors usually causes this fault to develop. One is poor coordination of the steps and the arm swing. The last step will start before the ball has reached the top of the backswing, in which case the bowler will

66. Forcing the forward swing

force the swing in order to catch up as illustrated in figure 66. This forcing of the forward swing causes her to drop the ball and also to lose her balance. The correction for this problem is explained in the section on carrying the ball. The forced forward swing may also be caused by a high backswing. It's not unusual for a too high backswing to cause a delay at the top, thus forcing the forward swing.

The other factor in causing a forced forward swing is the attempt to produce something "extra." This may be trying to apply more hook spin to the ball, or overemphasis on pitching the ball out onto the lane, or, frequently in the case of women, trying for added speed.

Dropping the ball, which causes the black marks on the runway behind the foul line, is caused in almost all cases by forcing or driving the forward swing. This is a vicious cycle in bowling. An experienced bowler will know when he is dropping the ball at the foul line; yet, when he tries to "really pitch the ball out" to correct his mistake, he will invariably force the forward swing and continue to drop the ball. The ball must be delivered out beyond the foul line *without unnecessary force* so that the fingers can apply the all-important split-second lift to the ball. Bowlers should constantly keep in mind that the ball is *rolled*, not thrown.

68. Forced forward swing corrected

The bowler in figure 67 was perfectly coordinated to the top of the back-swing; yet notice in the right-hand picture how the forced forward swing caused him to drop the ball behind the foul line. Forcing the forward swing also causes a stiffening of the left knee and that always spells trouble. Figure 68 shows the same bowler after the fault was corrected.

To correct a forced forward swing, first take your stance position and, without moving your feet, take a trial swing, saying to yourself (or counting along with the instructor) "one, two, three, *easy*." The speed of the count must be the same as the speed of the steps in your approach. After one or two trial swings, take your normal approach and deliver the ball. The counts of "one, two, three" will be synchronized with the first three steps, since no change will be made up to that point. Your problem is the forward swing. That is where you must remind yourself with to go easy as you start the ball down and through. Bring the ball down in the forward swing by its own weight and momentum; don't "muscle" it down. Figure 68 shows clearly the smooth forward swing, good balance, and pitching the ball out past the foul line that resulted when the bowler "reminded" himself with the simple word "easy."

If you are not able to make the correction using the above method, you will have to use the one-step delivery. The one-step delivery is the best cure for this problem, because forcing will cause a complete loss of balance. The bowler simply must ease up and *roll the ball* (stroke it) smoothly, in order to remain in balance. By alternating the one-step delivery and your regular approach and delivery, you should be able, in a few practice games, to eliminate this tendency to force the ball.

If you are having trouble delivering the ball out onto the lane, a simple measure that often works well is to remind yourself to hold onto the ball a split second longer than you have been doing. Using a towel for this practice as shown in figure 69 will also help. This exercise often eliminates the tendency to force the forward swing and consequently to drop the ball. Sometimes moving the target up closer (try the dots) eliminates the tendency to force the ball.

69. Delivering the ball
beyond the foul line

70. Ahead of the ball

Ahead of the Ball

All styles that appear to be ahead of the ball cannot be placed in the same category. A good bowler may have a normal, coordinated approach which brings him smoothly to the foul line where he plants himself firmly, then brings the ball down and through without effort or loss of control. This is a separate style not to be confused with the bowler who forces the downswing at the last second. The bowler in figure 70 does not have the coordination to bring the ball forward without forcing it, and he ends up dropping the ball. On the other hand, the bowler in figure 71 has complete control of the ball.

71. Perfect timing
from set position

Carrying the Ball

The mistake of carrying the ball is sometimes referred to as having a "loafed pendulum swing." This bothers not only beginners, who carry the ball because they are overcautious about remembering all the points of their game that they are trying to improve, but also many average bowlers as well, who get overcautious in a tight game. Even experienced bowlers sometimes get lazy on a simple shot, do not give full attention to their delivery and carry the ball.

Once the push-away has started, the ball must be kept in motion until it is released. You must not alter the speed of the natural pendulum swing by slowing the swing or by carrying the ball here and there along the swing. Usually the bowler who slows the swing or carries the ball during any part of the natural out-down-back-forward rhythm will find himself forcing the forward swing to catch up his timing. Forcing the forward swing in turn causes loss of timing, dropping the ball behind the foul line, dipping, side-wheeling, and a general off-balance delivery. (Remember always to fit the steps to the swing, not the swing to the steps.)

Carrying the ball also happens when bowlers, women more often than men, make the mistake of concentrating too much on laying the ball out onto the lane very smoothly. Too much emphasis on a smooth delivery can be a serious error, since it can cause the loss of much needed speed on the ball.

The bowler illustrated in figure 72 is completely out of time. Because he was too cautious with his swing, he carried the ball, causing the crooked arm and a forced forward swing.

72. Carrying the ball

73. Corrected timing

To correct the fault of carrying the ball, stand in the normal stance position and take a few trial swings until the swing is smooth and without hesitation. As you take these trial swings, count the swing rhythm to yourself—"one, two, three, four"—if you have a four-step approach, and "one, two, three" if you take three steps. Merely add a little zip to your push-away and down swing, and don't loaf or lag. You must have the smooth, rhythmic swing. The trial swing is definitely the cure for this problem. You should count in the same rhythm of your steps, so that your steps will fit in with your swing for perfect timing when you take off in your approach. Now take your regular approach and delivery, and count in the same rhythm as before. This should correct nearly all cases of carrying the ball. If not, you may need the assistance of your instructor as explained in figure 9b.

Although the bowler in figure 73 is just a beginner, his timing is now very good. You may notice that he is dropping the right knee too low, and his hand position could possibly be improved. Here again, the most prominent fault had to be corrected first. The bowler now has good timing, a higher backswing, and with it, the added natural speed that he formerly lacked.

8. THE DELIVERY

Failing to Face Straight Ahead

Facing straight ahead means having the shoulders perpendicular to a line from the bowler's right shoulder to the point of aim (see figure 74). This means that the shoulders are parallel with the foul line at the moment the ball is released. We say "face straight ahead" as a general direction, but the true meaning is "face straight towards your target with the shoulders perpendicular to the intended line of the ball." The target is still approached in a straight line from stance to foul line. In other words, the bowler is walking parallel to his line (the ball path) regardless of what angle he happens to be playing.

The value of perfect bowling form cannot be overemphasized. It is very important to have the trunk of the body lined up so that the right shoulder is directly over the intended path of the ball. Any style is satisfactory as long as you are able to do this. Figures 75a-b on the following page illustrate different styles which are both excellent.

74. Facing straight ahead

75. Facing straight ahead

Facing Straight Ahead

Keeping the right shoulder over the ball's line or path is emphasized even more when the bowler finds it necessary to play out and in, or belly the ball, as the bowler in figure 76 is doing. In this illustration, his line is the 15 board at the foul line to the 12 board at the arrows. Because of the perfect knee bend, balance, and the straight pendulum swing (stroke), he is able to place the ball perfectly over his intended line. It is obvious the bowler illustrated in figure 78 would have difficulty being consistent if he had to play this angle.

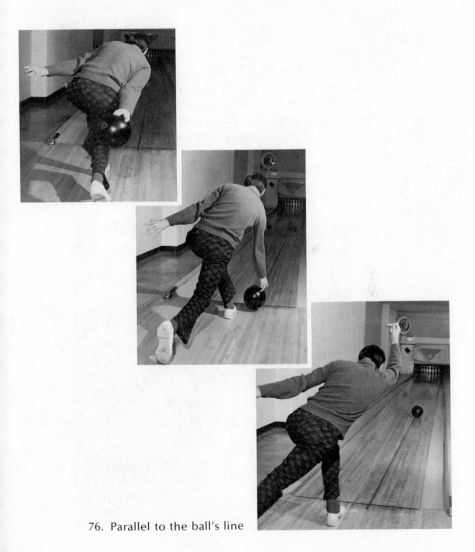

76. Parallel to the ball's line

This key fundamental is more evident when you study the picture of the bowler in figure 77 playing the 10-pin. Playing the left to right angle, notice how the body position has the right shoulder directly over the ball's intended line.

Incidentally, many people emphasize keeping the shoulder up as the ball is released. Actually, nearly all bowlers dip the right shoulder slightly as they release the ball, and that is not a fault, as seen by checking the bowler in figure 76. It is natural for the weight of the ball to pull the shoulder down to some degree. It is a fault and a problem, however, when the bowler *turns* and dips as the bowler in figure 82.

Facing straight ahead makes it easier to keep the pendulum swing on a straight line to the target than it is when the shoulders are turned, as they are in figure 78. This bowler cannot turn his shoulders exactly the same amount each time and therefore cannot be consistent or accurate. It is similar to shooting a rifle; you cannot shoot accurately if the rear sight moves to the left or right (see figure 79). In bowling, the right shoulder acts as the pivot point for the pendulum. Keeping the pivot point directly over the path intended for the ball will improve accuracy. The bowler who twists and turns at the foul line will invariably pull the ball. This causes the pendulum to swing at an angle instead of directly over the ball's path or intended line like the pendulum of a clock.

77. Playing the 10-pin

78. Shoulders not parallel
to the foul line

79. Inconsistent line of flight

80. Toes straight ahead

To correct the tendency to turn to the right as the ball is delivered, bend your left knee and put the weight of your body forward on your left foot. When emphasis is placed only on bending the left knee, many bowlers will rear back as they deliver the ball, losing their balance, which at best substitutes one fault for another. Do not bend the right knee. Keep the toe of the right shoe on the floor to act as a rudder and to prevent the right leg from swinging around to the left. A full rubber sole on the right shoe is an invaluable "brake" to stop the right leg from swinging to the left; a rubber tip on the toe of the shoe may be used for the same purpose. The bowler in figure 80 is the same bowler shown in figure 78 after the correction was made.

To correct the fault of not facing straight ahead, first take a dry run. If you cannot square the shoulders without the ball, you cannot do so with the ball. Take as many trial runs as you need until you feel that you are delivering the ball in balance and that your shoulders are squared away with the foul line.

The one-step delivery, explained in detail in section 1, is the best cure for correction of poor delivery form. To work on a problem that requires the dry run and the one-step delivery, bowl on a lane away from other bowlers, without the pins if possible. First, take a one-step delivery by yourself. While you wait for the ball to return, take a dry run. Then take your complete approach and deliver the ball. Repeat this sequence until the shoulders are parallel to the foul line at the moment of releasing the ball.

You can check yourself by looking straight down over your front knee *after* releasing the ball. If your toes point straight ahead, you are in balance and facing straight ahead. Notice how many of the top bowlers pose momentarily after releasing the ball, as shown in figure 81. It is very easy for this bowler to check his balance and be sure he is facing straight ahead.

81. Pose after releasing the ball

Loss of Balance during the Delivery

Balance during the delivery depends on the left knee bend (the right knee for left-handers), toes pointed straight ahead, and the weight of the body shifted almost entirely to the front foot. Proper balance and facing straight ahead are closely related. In general, a bowler who faces straight ahead will maintain his balance throughout the delivery. Therefore, the method used to correct flaws in balance is the same as that used for failure to face straight ahead, which was discussed at the beginning of this section.

Good balance as the ball is delivered is important in several ways. Aside from the obvious problems that loss of balance can cause, it contributes to other faults, such as side-wheeling, dropping the shoulder, turning to the right (to the left for left-handers), and many others. You will even find bowlers who complain that their foot sticks as they attempt to slide to the foul line. This trouble can be traced to loss of balance. The left heel has made firm contact with the approach instead of allowing the slide to continue on the sole of the shoe.

Bear in mind that you build up considerable momentum during the approach. An unbalanced delivery makes it very difficult to stop smoothly behind the foul line. Bend the front knee, and the upper part of the body will carry forward automatically. This delivery form also will eliminate lofting the ball, since the ball will be released only a few inches above the floor.

82. Loss of balance during delivery

83. Instructor encouraging the follow-through

84. Balance maintained
throughout delivery

The bowler illustrated in figures 82–84 is a very good example of "before" and "after" delivery form. It doesn't require much work, just a little patience and understanding of the value of sound delivery fundamentals, to develop the proper form. In this case, the one-step delivery corrected the fault. Figure 83 shows the instructor working with the bowler. This help was necessary to encourage the follow-through that he did not have at first. The "after" picture, figure 84, speaks for itself.

Lofting the Ball

Lofting the ball is what we call throwing the ball several feet beyond the foul line from a nearly standing position. Aside from being very hard on the lanes, from the bowler's viewpoint it is objectionable because it does not produce good ball roll and action. Because the ball does not have time enough to "grab" the lane, it skids too much after it is lofted.

Lofting generally is caused by the ball being too light, or the thumb hole being too tight, or the bowler not bending the front knee in his delivery. A different ball will correct the first two causes of lofting. To correct the third cause (not bending the front knee), the simple one-step delivery is the cure.

Crooked Pendulum Swing

To correct a crooked pendulum swing, first make certain that your delivery form is satisfactory: bent left knee, body weight forward on the left foot, facing straight ahead. If your delivery form is correct, the fault causing the crooked pendulum swing will be found in one or more of the following places: in the push-away and downswing; in the backswing, by bringing the ball behind the body; in the backswing, by bringing the ball back out away from the body, or to the right of the desired pendulum.

If the fault is in the push-away or downswing, it is not too difficult to correct. If your ball is near the center of the body in the stance position, take a trial swing and make certain you push the ball slightly *right and down*. Repeat this several times, checking the position of your hand (do not turn your wrist) as you drop the arm into the downswing. If when you deliver the ball you still make the mistakes, try the stance position shown in figure 4a, making certain your elbow is snug against your side.

If this does not correct it, your instructor will help by steering the ball during the trial swing (see figure 85). If necessary, the instructor can take the first and second steps with you and then step aside, as he is doing with the bowler in figure 85b. Several deliveries like this should correct even the extreme cases.

The error of bringing the ball behind the body during the backswing is the most prevalent of the crooked pendulums (see figure 86a). Many good bowlers make this mistake, but they do it consistently. However, they are the exceptions, and if the fault is corrected at an early stage, any bowler will be much better off.

85. Correcting a crooked pendulum swing

86. Two crooked pendulums

The bowler shown in figure 86b brings the ball out and away from the body in the backswing. To correct this error, first make certain that the backswing is not too high. Next, stand about four feet behind the foul line and take a trial swing. Keep your eyes on the arm all the way back into the backswing. Lower your head in order to watch the arm (see figure 49b). When you feel you are swinging the ball in a straight pendulum, take the one-step delivery and release the ball. After five or six one-step deliveries, try alternating the one-step delivery with the complete approach. Repeat these alternately until the fault is corrected. If you have difficulty keeping the arm straight even in the one-step delivery, your instructor can help you as shown in figure 87.

87. Correcting a bent arm

Arm Twisting

This section applies only to beginners who twist the arm in the pendulum swing. Girls and women sometimes do not have the necessary strength to keep the arm straight. Many experienced bowlers and some top stars deliberately or through habit turn the arm in the backswing so that the palm is up at the top of the backswing. When this has become part of their style and they are able to do it consistently under all conditions, it presents no problem. Nevertheless, the beginner who twists the arm during the delivery should correct the fault immediately.

To make this correction, first make certain your ball fits you perfectly and is the correct weight. Then in the stance position take several trial swings, checking your hand position to make sure that both hands are under the ball. Watch your hand closely as the ball starts down from the push-away. If you can avoid arm twisting during the trial swing, you should be able to take your approach and delivery and release the ball without the arm twisting. If not, you may have to call your instructor for assistance as shown in figures 9b and 87.

88. Twisting the arm

Figure 88 shows a bowler who twists the arm in the backswing. The instructor is shown catching the ball in the trial swing so that the bowler can turn around and see where the mistake was made. Notice that the arm twist encourages the additional fault of turning the shoulders. Use the trial swing and watch your hand position carefully to correct arm twisting in the push-away, the downswing, and the backswing.

If you twist the arm during the forward swing, a different method of correction is necessary. Stand at the head of the approach (see figure 89) with your instructor standing at the foul line. Roll the ball down the approach, concentrating on keeping the arm rigid; follow through completely so that you are able to sight over your thumb as you point to your target. Repeat this procedure until the fault is fully corrected. When you are able to bring the ball out, down, back, and forward with your arm rigid and straight, take your normal approach and deliver the ball.

In extreme cases you may have to ask your instructor to hold your wrist during the one-step delivery, or even to go through the entire approach and delivery with you, as illustrated in figure 90.

89. Correction for twisting the arm

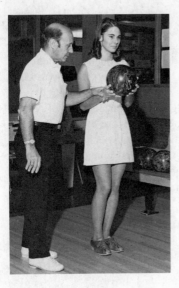

90. Instructor assisting in complete
approach and delivery

The High Backswing

The high backswing is not in itself a fault. Although a high backswing is not recommended for men, there is nothing wrong with it provided the bowler has both good approach timing and delivery form and proper ball speed. Many high-average bowlers, including champions, use a high backswing.

A higher backswing is recommended for women, however, because it gives added speed without unnecessary force or strain. The average woman bowler can use additional speed, but not at the expense of timing or delivery form. If the high backswing causes the hips or shoulders to turn, the bowler should change to a lower backswing. The pivoting will cause dipping of the right shoulder and even side-wheeling, two faults that would not be worth the speed gained.

A delay at the top of the backswing could be caused by a high backswing, and this is also not worth the additional speed to be gained.

The bowler illustrated in figure 91 displays good timing and delivery form in spite of the high backswing. Figure 92 shows the recommended backswing. Figure 93 shows a bowler who has a high backswing, but he also has too much speed and a small timing problem. He will have to lower the backswing.

To make this correction, first consider timing; a lower stance position may be necessary, or the number of steps may have to be changed. These should be tried first. If they do not do the job, ask your instructor for assistance. First take your trial swing from about four feet behind the foul line (as in figure 94a). As

91. High backswing with proper speed and timing

92. Recommended backswing

93. High backswing with excessive speed and poor timing

94. Correcting the
high backswing

you take these trial swings, the instructor will stand beside you. He will slap the ball at the correct height, and as you swing he will count aloud in the rhythm of your approach.

From this same position on the runway, take a one-step delivery, again counting the cadence of your steps. Concentrate on the proper height of the backswing, then on bringing the ball forward, down, and through on the last count. You should have the feel of where the ball is at all times during the count, especially on the last two counts.

Do not hurry this exercise. When you are able to take the one-step delivery without assistance so that it feels easy and smooth, try a dry run or two. Then make your full approach while your instructor watches so that he can call a halt if he sees that you are about to revert to your old style. Figure 94b-c show the bowler of figure 93 after he has corrected his high backswing. His backswing is lower, he is relaxed, his knees are bent, and his timing is better. This same technique will correct a hesitation in the backswing.

A Hop in the Delivery

Figures 95a-b clearly show this fault. This kind of hop during the delivery is not uncommon, and some bowlers with respectable averages have one. But this certainly is not the easy way to bowl. This bowler delivers the ball well behind the foul line, his timing is off a little, and obviously he must hop to keep from falling.

Correction of this fault is not difficult. Alternate the dry run and the one-step delivery, if possible without using the pins, and concentrate on bending the knee. Figure 95c shows the same bowler after he eliminated the hop from his delivery.

95. Correcting the hop for balance

A Wide Pendulum Swing (Side-wheeling)

The inconsistency and inaccuracy that occur because of a wide pendulum swing (side-wheeling) are illustrated in the "before and after" pictures of the same bowler shown in figure 96.

This style is not unusual, especially with young bowlers. The teenage boy generally learns to bowl with a ball that is heavier than it should be while he is learning; he usually trys to put that "extra stuff" on the ball. The ball simply pulls him down because he is not strong enough at this stage to control it.

This phase of delivery form is associated with facing straight ahead, which was discussed at the beginning of this section. Check and compare figure 96a with figure 74. It is obvious that the bowler who can deliver the ball with his arm directly over and on a line with his target will hit his target more consistently. To correct this error, use the methods described for learning to face straight ahead. Alternate the dry run with the one-step delivery.

96. Correcting side-wheeling

97. Correcting the wide pendulum swing

(a) Wide pendulum swing

(b & c) Corrected swing

It helps considerably in the correction of this fault to move temporarily to the extreme outside of the approach to the first arrow. Crowding the channel will force you to keep your arm closer to your side. The bowler shown in figure 97a is a very good example of a wide pendulum swing. Figures 97b-c show the same bowler playing the *outside angle* to make the correction. If possible, work on correcting this fault without pins, since any tendency to notice the pins or move in will cause you to revert to your old habit of side-wheeling.

(a) Dumping the ball

98. Correcting a poor
    follow-through

(b)   Reaching for the ceiling

A Poor Follow-through

The follow-through and its value were explained in section 3. Good timing and delivery form generally ensure a good follow-through, although there are exceptions. Figure 98a shows a bowler whose timing and delivery form are satisfactory, yet she cuts off her follow-through by dumping the ball, thereby impairing her accuracy, ball roll, and the added natural speed generated by the follow-through.

To correct a poor follow-through, try the one-step delivery and "reach for the ceiling"; let your right arm continue all the way up to your right ear. After a few practice rolls you should be able to follow through correctly.

If this does not do the job, ask your instructor to stand on the return as illustrated in figure 98b. A few attempts at "shaking hands" in this manner will remind you to get the arm up where it belongs on the follow-through.

(c) Lunging

(d) A perfect finish

The opposite of dumping the ball is displayed by the bowler in figure 98c. Trying for that extra something on the ball will usually cause the bowler to lunge. "Shaking hands" will correct this problem too. Aim for the finishing position shown in figure 98d.

9. BALL ROLL

Proper Ball Speed

All bowlers must roll a ball from the foul line to the pins in 2-1/8 to 2-3/4 seconds if they are to get the maximum benefit of pin action. The average male bowler rolls the ball from the foul line to the pins in 2-1/4 to 2-1/2 seconds. Any roll that is faster than this is too fast, since the fast ball cannot get enough traction on the lane to "dig in" in its last ten to twenty feet before hitting the pocket. Rolling a ball too fast is like trying to get your car out of the mud by spinning its wheels at a furious rate instead of turning them slowly to use what friction you can. The ball that is delivered too slowly has other disadvantages. In most cases, all hook spin will have been dissipated by the time the ball reaches the pins. The "too slow" ball is common for women, especially when they are learning and during their first few games.

To increase your ball speed, change to the chin-high stance described earlier. This will give you a longer pendulum and a higher backswing. You might even try pushing the ball out and slightly up in order to get a longer arc. Past experience proves that this not only adds natural speed, but that the higher push-away often develops a better stroke.

Some bowlers, however, will lose their timing with this type of push-away. They can get additional speed by "kicking" the ball into the push-away and down-swing with a little more zip. This tends to speed up both the arm swing and the steps automatically. Do not try this without your instructor's assistance. He will observe this closely to prevent you from fouling up your timing. "Kicking" the ball could easily cause you to develop a "three-step swing with a four-step approach." Your instructor's count and close observation of the coordination of arm and feet will determine the cadence of your steps.

Do not try for added speed by forcing the forward swing or by trying to raise the height of the backswing. The higher backswing must come naturally from either of the two methods described above.

This is about all you can do for the present. The natural speed you want can only be gained by improvement in coordination, which takes practice and patience to develop.

Women should roll a ball from the foul line to the pocket in three seconds or less. However, this is easier said than done. Women should not try for additional speed by deliberately trying to overpower the pins. If four seconds is the best a pupil can do—fine! That is her natural speed and it will have to do as a beginning.

The "too fast" ball can be difficult to correct, assuming the bowler has natural speed and is not forcing. To slow down the fast ball, the bowler should concentrate on *rolling* the ball instead of throwing it. This will often slow everything down, yet maintain timing and coordination. If this does not work, he can reduce the height of the backswing, or lower the position of the ball in the stance position. Bear in mind that the shorter the length of the arc, the slower the ball will be delivered if it is not forced. If these changes do not work, concentrate on the speed of the approach. To slow down the approach speed, count your steps in a slower cadence, "one, two, three, four," which should do the job. Make this change carefully because slowing the steps can otherwise result in loss of timing. While it is advantageous to reduce the speed of the extremely fast ball, it must be done without impairment of natural timing and coordination. Otherwise you may have corrected one fault at the expense of introducing several others more burdensome than the "too fast" delivery.

Killing the Hook

Not getting the hook is called "killing the hook." This can be caused by several things. Generally the hand is not in the proper position as the ball is released (see section 5). To roll an effective hook, the fingers *must* be between the 3 and 5 o'clock positions as the ball is released, preferably at 4 to 4:30 o'clock. Any other hand position will result in either a straight ball, a near-straight ball, a back-up, or a reverse hook.

Even when the fingers are in the proper position, "dumping" the ball on the lane will kill the hook. Dumping the ball is a term for releasing the ball with the fingers and thumb at the same time (see figure 99a). Imagine that you are holding a suitcase by its handle and that you want to slide it down the lane to the pins without the suitcase falling over on its side. In order to accomplish this unlikely objective, you would have to release the handle with the fingers and thumb at the same time. If you dump the ball in this way, a follow-through with a pronounced bend of the elbow will remind you to lift and not to dump the ball (see figure 99b).

(b) Bending the elbow

(a) Dumping

99. Correction for dumping the ball

To roll an effective hook, the thumb must leave the ball first; then the fingers apply the hook spin. Like the pro golfer who can feel the club head hit the ball, the bowler must develop the feel of the fingers lifting the ball the split-second it is released. The good bowler concentrates on the position of the fingers and the lift, not on the position of the thumb or thumb hole, because it is easier to visualize the fingers lifting than the correct position of the thumb.

Figure 100 shows a bowler who has not maintained the correct hand position throughout the delivery. He has applied finger lift to the ball, but he has turned the wrist clockwise so that the lift was from the inside at about 7 o'clock instead of from the outside at about 4 to 5 o'clock. He has rolled a back-up despite the lift by the fingers. The fingers must be on the outside to roll the hook ball.

To correct these faults you must learn to roll the conventional (stiff wrist) hook, not the "turn and lift" type. Any maneuver other than a stiff wrist will make correction difficult. Therefore lock your wrist in a stiff position with the middle and ring fingers at 4 o'clock, as illustrated in figure 48. Next, bring the ball up to your starting position, keeping the grip firm so that the wrist will remain rigid and straight. Take several trial swings, observing the wrist and hand closely to make certain the wrist is rigid and the hand is in the proper position (see figure 49b). Take the one-step delivery. Repeat this procedure until the

100. Turning the wrist

hand position is completely satisfactory and you can feel the ball coming off the two fingers as you lift straight up.

If you are unable to release the ball correctly and you revert to your old fault, call on your instructor for assistance (see figure 87). You will soon get the feel and develop proper wrist position if he holds your wrist in this manner.

Marking the ball with tape as illustrated in section 11 will assist in checking the amount of "turn and finish" on the ball, as well as the position of the ball track, the surface on which the ball rolls. A three- or four-inch piece of white tape directly under the finger holes will show the amount of turn or spin on the ball. The properly released hook ball will clearly show an acceleration of spin by the tape the last ten to twenty feet before the ball hits the pins. This is referred to as a good *finishing* ball. It will have a minimum of deflection upon contact with the head pin.

Study the excellent pictures of the fingers coming out of the ball, figure 53. This type of release and hand position will get you the desired twelve or thirteen complete revolutions from the foul line to the pocket.

Too Much Hook or Curve

A combination of a light ball and insufficient speed will cause too much hook or curve. Therefore, this is more often a problem for women bowlers; men generally have enough strength and speed to keep the ball from "running away," even with excessive hook spin.

For the woman who rolls a light ball slowly down the lane, this can be a big problem. Assuming that everything possible has been done to increase natural speed, and that a ten-pound ball is the heaviest she can handle, she will have to be content with these conditions for the present. The amount of curve can be reduced by straightening out the hand and wrist so that the thumb is in the 11:30 o'clock position, just enough to give the ball a slight lift with the fingers without any wrist turn. It is usually best for all bowlers to roll a hook, and it is to be regretted if one loses a natural hook. However, there is no alternative if the hook simply curves beyond control, no matter from what angle it is rolled from the foul line.

To change the hand position so that the thumb is at the 11:30 o'clock position, stand at the head of the approach and roll the ball to your instructor standing at the foul line (see figure 36). Repeat the procedure until you are able to keep the wrist straight and rigid, then roll one down the lane. Repeat the entire procedure until you are able to deliver the ball consistently, thereby cutting down the amount of curve. Watch out for overcorrection, which will produce the back-up, which is always a possibility when the thumb position approaches the 11:30 or 12 o'clock position.

III

Advanced Techniques
and
Technical Information

10. Taps and Splits

Taps

When a bowler appears to do everything right—good approach timing, good delivery, good hook rolled solidly into the pocket—and still leaves a pin, that is a *tap*. As long as the game of bowling survives, you will hear bowlers lament the taps that robbed them of the big score.

In the following picture sequences, you will notice the painted white lines that border the general pocket area, that is, boards 16, 17, and 18 from the right channel. These lines allow you to follow better the deflection of the ball or lack of it.

The ball travels approximately 10-1/2 inches from contact with the head pin until it hits the 3-pin. A slight deflection in this critical area makes a 10-pin tap possible, regardless of the angle at which the ball came into the pocket. Surprisingly, the angle played by the bowler makes very little difference in the pin fall pattern.

Figure 101 illustrates the 10-pin tap. This is the most common tap for right-handed bowlers. Figure 101a clearly shows the ball hitting the pocket dead center (on the 17 board). Figure 101b shows the ball deflecting approximately one-half inch after it made contact with the head pin. The mere one-half inch of deflection is enough to cause the 10-pin tap. A solid hit like this will produce a strike most of the time. Unfortunately, the bowler did something different on this roll and the ball deflected.

Illustrated in figure 102 is another solid pocket hit, but this one carried for a strike. This hit also was on the 17 board, the center of the pocket. In comparing the two hits, the only apparent difference is the one-half inch of deflection on the 10-pin leave, whereas the strike shows the ball hitting the head pin and then driving straight back without deflecting.

101. The 10-pin tap

102. Solid pocket hit for a strike

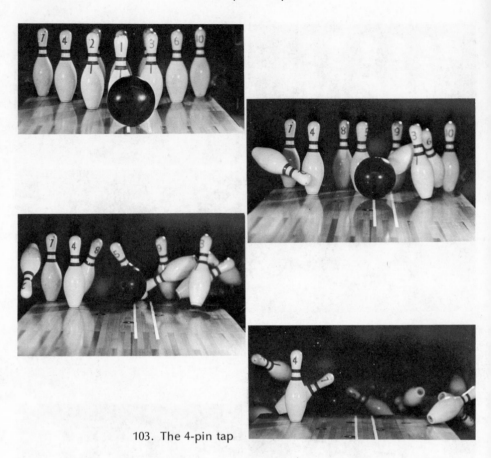

103. The 4-pin tap

Illustrated in figure 103 is a solid 4-pin tap. This particular roll was on the 18 board when it made contact with the head pin. Although "high" hits like this are hardly detected with the naked eye, it is obvious that the ball hit high when you analyze the pin fall pattern. The pattern differs considerably from the 10-pin leave, and the ball came in just one board higher. All high hits like this 4-pin leave show the head pin must take out the 9-pin, with the 2-pin coming off the kickback to get the 4- and 7-pins. It is simply a matter of luck it seems; sometimes they fall, but sometimes they narrowly miss being hit, as they did in this sequence.

The solid 8-pin tap leaves no room for argument. All experts agree that the solid 8-pin leave is a tap. As illustrated in figure 104, the hit was solid and the ball was digging hard and fast into the pocket.

This tap is caused by the 5-pin chopping (*cherrying off*) the 8-pin. This cherry comes about because an "assist" from the head pin gives the 5-pin a glancing blow, sending it to the right and missing the 8-pin. On most strikes, the head pin

104. The 8-pin tap

hits the 2-pin a glancing blow, then goes straight back with the ball, hitting the five-pin, the 8-pin or both.

You doubtless will hear the statement made that "it was the wrong angle to carry the 10-pin" (or the 4-pin). We don't believe that one angle is much better than another. Where is the angle that will not leave a tap? At best, changing the angle may possibly increase the chance of carrying one particular pin, but it will also decrease the chance of carrying another. All that will have been accomplished is a substitution of one pin for another. However, bowlers can play a good tight line and leave just as many corner pins on good hits as bowlers who play down the fifth board and into the pocket. If a bowler has more confidence from one particular angle than from another, that is the place from which he should roll. Bluntly, put your faith in hitting the pocket solidly rather than in the place the ball is rolled from. For the beginner and average bowler, the second arrow is the recommended target for rolling the strike ball, but if you have more confidence in moving a few boards either way, by all means do so.

105. Light pocket hit

Pocket Splits and Deflection

All bowlers—champion, average, beginner—will leave pocket splits. They will also hit the 1–3 pocket and leave the 5-pin, or the 5–8 pins due to the deflection of the ball on contact with pins. Bowlers with better timing and better hook spin and roll on the ball will not run into the pocket split as often as the bowler with poorer timing and the poorer ball. We could also add that incorrect angle "encourages" the pocket split; a straight ball rolled down the center of the lane instead of off the right-hand corner, for example, or a hook played from too far inside, when the bowler does not roll a hook strong enough to combat the deflection encountered. This is especially true if the lanes are a little "fast" (slick) and the

106. Pocket split

pins are on the heavy side. Figure 105 shows what looked to be a good pocket hit, but the ball "quit" (deflected to the right). On a normal strike pattern, the ball hits enough of the 5-pin to drive it into the 8-pin. Any time a bowler, strong hook or average hook, hits the pocket and leaves the 5–7, 5–10, or single 5-pin, it is simply a case of the ball quitting when it hit the 1–3.

The pocket hit shown in figure 105 was considered a little light, the ball coming in on the 16 board. However, if it had been a good roll the ball would not have deflected over two inches as this one did. The ball must be right of the 14 board in order to miss the 5-pin.

The 8–10 split in figure 106 was left by a hit dead center in the pocket (17 board). On this particular roll, the bowler simply rolled a bad ball.

Other Splits and What to Do about Them

The pocket split is usually caused by a poorly rolled ball, whereas the other splits come from errors of accuracy—usually high on the head pin, or "right on the nose." All splits are provoking, but they are part of the game. Even the best hitters in baseball will hit into a double play now and then.

Unless the game depends on the conversion of the split, we suggest playing it safe by always getting one pin (or two pins in the case of splits like the 6–7–10). Many a game is lost by one or two pins. If you have a strike preceding the split, *always* get at least half of the split with the second roll. If you should attempt the conversion of the 6–7–10 and get too wide and drop into the channel, you will lose four pins in count. You should, of course, always attempt to make the "little" splits like the 3–10, 4–5 because any reasonable attempt will get at least one pin.

If you or your team is down by a considerable margin in a match or game, then go for broke and try to convert your splits, much as a baseball team trailing by a big margin will go for the big inning, rather than sacrifice to get one run.

One last suggestion: never try to convert the railroads (4–6, 7–10, 8–10, 7–9) by sliding one pin into the other. The chance of this type of conversion is very remote, and you will often miss both pins and lose count for your score. The percentage is better if you try to hit one pin a solid blow, slamming it into the ball cushion in the rear of the pit, hoping that it will carom off and into the other pin.

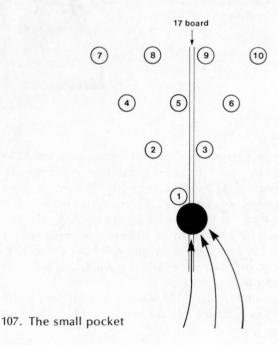

107. The small pocket

Which Angle is Best to Play?

In the series of pin action shots, we have attempted to prove that we must accept the facts that the pocket is small (see figure 107) and that bowling is a highly skilled sport. We must also acknowledge that we roll the bowling ball sixty feet down a lane and try to hit an area less than two inches wide. When we hit the pocket but the ball wasn't rolling very well, we are subjected to taps and splits. It is truly a game of fractions. A quarter-inch or less can be the difference between glory and frustration. We can, however, play the percentages.

The pin action shown in figures 101–106 proves that deflection causes the 10-pin tap, and excessive deflection causes the pocket splits and the 5-pin leave. Obviously, then, the extreme outside angle as illustrated in figure 108 will produce less deflection than the inside or tight line angle. Therefore, the inside angle, or tight line, is only for the bowler who rolls a very strong ball, as the bowler in figure 57.

108. Tight, normal, and outside angles

The bowler in figure 109 is playing the *outside* line or angle. This angle is definitely better for the slight hook and the straight ball; it is especially good for the woman who does not have much power.

The beginner who plays this angle should be very careful of the tendency to drift to the left. If the bowler shown here were to drift a board or two to the left, he might hit his target, but the ball would not come up to the pocket. Specifically, the bowler in figure 109 places his ball on the third board at the foul line, and his target is the first range finder (the fifth board). But if he placed the ball on the fifth board at the foul line and hit the *same* target, the ball would not come up to the head pin.

When you have determined the angle of your ball's path, have your instructor or a teammate check whether or not you are placing the ball on the proper foul line board. You have to rely on their observation since you cannot see this—you are looking at your target.

109. Playing the outside angle

11. DIFFERENT TYPES OF BALL ROLL

All bowlers will roll one of the following types of balls: straight ball, full roller, semi-roller, semi-spinner, full spinner, back-up or reverse hook. Nearly all average and better-than-average bowlers will roll either the full roller or the semi-roller. The various types of rolls are pictured on the following pages. Two photographs of each type show the instant the ball is released. The tape is parallel to the ball track, the surface on which the ball contacts the lane. Notice the difference in the position and width of the tracks.

Straight Ball

Figure 110 shows the straight ball. Notice that the hand is in back of, or behind, the ball as it is released. The thumb is pointed to approximately 11:30 o'clock as the ball is released, and the ball rolls down the lane like a wheel. The bowler who rolls a straight ball must be certain to keep the thumb and fingers in these positions the instant the ball is released. It is easy for the thumb to slip beyond the 12 o'clock position, and the result is the undesirable back-up.

The straight ball is not recommended for men. We do, however, recommend a straight ball for a woman who lacks ball speed. The slower the ball, the lighter the ball, the more it will curve. Excessive curve would make accuracy a problem in a hook ball.

The straight ball, then, is for the woman who should not be rolling a hook. However, it should be rolled from the corner, as in figure 110b. Take advantage of the angle into the pocket to increase your strike chances. It is obvious that the ball will deflect less if it comes into the pocket from the outside.

110. The straight ball

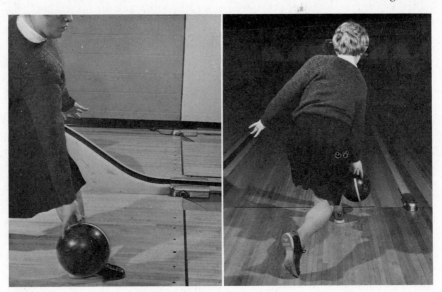

Full Roller

Approximately ten percent of the top bowlers roll the full roller. It differs from the straight ball only in the position of the thumb and fingers at the instant the ball is released. The fingers lift the straight ball from behind (5:30 to 6 o'clock), whereas the fingers lift the full roller from the side (3 to 5 o'clock). This lift from the side imparts the hook spin, which causes the ball to curve as it travels down the lane. Since the straight ball and the full roller differ only in the position of the thumb and fingers at the instant of release, it is obvious that the straight ball bowler need only move the fingers around to the side of the ball as he releases it in order to roll a hook ball. Notice that the ball track covers the full circumference of the ball, hence the name full roller. The track is from one-fourth to one inch wide. (see figure 115).

Semi-roller

This is the most popular of the hook balls. For the full roller, the axis of rotation is parallel to the lane surface. For the semi-roller (also known as a three-quarters roller), the axis is tilted somewhat, which causes the ball to roll on a track below the thumb hole. The semi-roller ball track will also be less than a full circumference of the ball.

Many bowlers consider the semi-roller to be the strongest hook ball, but it is the bowler's ability to impart split-second lift with good timing that determines the effectiveness of any hook ball. There are many weak and strong hook balls in both the full roller and semi-roller categories.

The difference in the full roller and the semi-roller stems from the lift imparted by the fingers. Notice the angle or direction in which the fingers apply the lift in the semi-roller (figure 111). Also notice how the wrist is slightly "cocked" or broken, causing a tilt in the axis of rotation. By contrast, the full roller is given lift straight up.

111. The semi-roller

112. The semi-spinner

Semi-spinner

Many bowlers use the term semi-spinner and semi-roller interchangeably. We use the term *roller* to refer to a ball in which the hook spin is applied by a lift with the fingers, with wrist turn a secondary factor. For the *spinners,* the turn of the wrist is essential to apply a spin, with finger lift the secondary factor.

In any event, the difference between the semi-roller and semi-spinner can be seen when you compare the position of the ball track. For the semi-spinner, the wider or cone-shaped track is caused by applying more wrist turn, along with the lift by the fingers (figure 112).

It is natural for some bowlers to roll the wrist a bit counterclockwise as they release the ball. Others deliberately turn the wrist, as illustrated in figure 54.

Full Spinner

This is the weakest of the hook balls, and it is not recommended. At best, it is only moderately effective on slow or running lanes and is practically lost on faster lanes and heavier pins.

The full spinner is released as illustrated in figure 113, with the wrist turning counterclockwise from directly on top of the ball. Little or no finger action is employed, and the ball travels down the lane spinning like a top.

113. The full spinner

Why anyone chooses to roll the full spinner is puzzling. Perhaps bowlers who roll this ball are trying to roll the turn and lift type hook but have not developed the finger lift, only the wrist turn.

Back-up or Reverse Hook

Contrary to accepted beliefs, there is a distinct difference between a back-up and a reverse hook. The back-up is actually intended to be a straight ball (see section 3), but because the bowler releases the ball with the fingers coming up a little to the left of center, the ball will fade to the right. The ball moving to the right is similar to the reverse hook, but the reverse hook is thrown with a deliberate clockwise lift by the fingers. This is the same procedure that hook ball bowlers follow for natural lift, except that the lift is from the opposite side of the ball.

We have known a few better-than-average reverse hook bowlers. The bowler illustrated in figure 114 rolls a very strong ball. But the question is, why release the ball unnaturally when a natural hook lift is easier and so much better? For those reverse hook bowlers who claim it is natural for them, here is a simple demonstration to disprove their theory. Stand with your hands at your sides and notice how your thumb points inward toward the body. Swing the arms forward and notice how the fingers remain on the outside as you bring the arms up. This is the natural hook lift. The opposite, or unnatural, happens when the fingers flip from the inside, or clockwise, for a right-hander.

114. The reverse hook

Modern bowling equipment has eliminated the ball return that stretches the full length of the approach. This gives the reverse hook bowler more room for his body when bowling from the left side; even so, the reverse hook is not recommended, because it is more difficult to roll and to control consistently. No bowler should roll from the left side of the approach and shoot for the 1–2 pocket when the right side and the 1–3 pocket is easier and more natural.

How the Ball Rolls

The ball illustrated in figure 115 is a full roller. The ball track is between the two taped lines. The speed of this ball is medium.

Notice that the ball skids forward approximately sixteen feet before any effect of the hook spin is noticed. This is much like a car skidding on ice, even though the front wheels may be turned. The skid is entirely the result of the momentum of the ball. The effect of lane friction begins to show in figure 115c causing the track of the ball to turn and start into the forward roll. Lane friction is a constant factor on the full length of the lane. Once the ball begins to change direction, the hook spin changes the direction at an ever-increasing rate. This accounts for the ball "breaking" from right to left in the last ten to twenty feet of its journey. The hooking action of a bowling ball is similar to acceleration in physics. Once acceleration (hook spin) has started, the velocity (curve of the ball) will continue to increase.

115. A full roller

116. A semi-roller

Bowlers tend to be impressed with the number of turns or revolutions a ball makes as it rolls down the lane and into the pocket. No doubt trying for this extra turn is the reason so many bowlers (especially the teen-age stars) develop the turn and lift type hook.

A good hook ball delivered with average speed will generally make eight to ten complete turns from leaving the bowler's hand until it hits the pocket. The full roller illustrated in figure 115 makes twelve complete revolutions.

The ball illustrated in figure 116 is a semi-roller. Notice that the track is below the thumb hole. The speed of this ball is medium-fast. This ball makes thirteen to fourteen complete revolutions from the foul line to the pins. The number of turns alone, however, does not necessarily make a ball powerful. The more effective ball depends entirely on the relationship between the turns and the speed. A ball can turn eight times and be a good strike ball if it is delivered at the proper speed. On the other hand, a ball with thirteen or more turns may be only mediocre as a strike getter if it is rolled too fast or too slow, or if the bowler's timing is such that the ball is not delivered out onto the lane naturally.

12. TEACHING SENIOR CITIZENS AND CHILDREN

Bowling is promoted as a sport for the ages of six to eighty-six, and everyone can learn to bowl the correct and most comfortable way. The most important consideration for senior citizens learning to bowl is safety. A fall for many at this age could be serious. Figure 117 illustrates the best method for teaching senior citizens.

The one-step delivery without the ball is the first operation. The instructor must make certain that the pupil understands the coordination of the swing with

117. Teaching the senior citizen

the step. After eight or ten complete simulated deliveries as shown, have the pupil try it with the ball. For the first attempt at rolling the ball, I suggest the instructor remain at the bowler's side, as shown in figure 117d. Confusion or excitement may cause loss of coordination and a possible stumble. The instructor should stand by to prevent any mishaps.

Figures 117e-f show the beginning bowler making the complete delivery on his own. Not only will he enjoy the sport, he will be able to score well with this one-step style. To change later to a three-step approach, refer to section 1.

Teaching Children

Teaching boys and girls from the ages of six to ten is not a problem if you follow the procedure outlined in figure 118. I do not recommend teaching the approach at this time, no matter how light the ball may be. Rushing things would do more harm than good.

Have the students pick up the ball with both hands, as shown in figure 118a, and carry it to the foul line (figure 118b). Then, tell them to set the ball down and position themselves comfortably (figure 118c). Next, have them bring the ball back (figure 118d), then down and forward (figure 118e).

This method makes the swing easy for them, and they will learn proper balance and to face straight ahead at the same time they are knocking down pins, which is their biggest concern. Depending on their age and strength, the biggest problem is trying to keep the arm from twisting. If necessary, the instructor or a parent can hold the wrist as shown in figure 87. If the child has his own ball, this can be practiced at home by rolling the ball on the carpet. Before going further, I emphasize: *Do not rush things.* Keep the children bowling in this manner until they have developed better balance, and most important the straight arm and hand position. Their scoring will improve automatically as they develop the proper form.

When this skill is mastered, the children are ready to initiate the normal instructional sequence (one-step, three-step, four-step) beginning on page 12.

118. Teaching children to bowl

13. SOME TECHNICAL INFORMATION

Equipment

In every competitive sport it is necessary to have your own equipment, custom-fitted to your own dimensions, in order to achieve your maximum performance. The golfer needs his own clubs; the baseball player his own glove and a bat that feels just right; the bowler should have his own equipment—especially a ball that is custom-fitted to his own hand. Using improperly tailored equipment in baseball or golf will usually result only in a mediocre performance, but an ill-fitting bowling ball can cause physical damage such as blisters, swollen fingers and knuckles and pulled muscles in addition to a sub-par performance. Every bowler should purchase a custom-fitted bowling ball at the earliest opportunity. It is a small premium to pay for the extra enjoyment of the game. Bowling shoes and a bowling bag complete the outfit of very desirable custom equipment. Bowlers should wear loose comfortable clothing that allows freedom of movement.

Ball Pitch

Most bowlers have a special grip that they have designed, and each has his own reasons for not using the conventional grip. Figure 119a shows the standard three-eighths inch pitch of the conventional three-hole grip. This is the design recommended by nearly all instructors, particularly for beginning bowlers.

Figure 119b shows a center drilling called zero pitch. The conventional drilling has a forward pitch three-eighths of an inch above the center of the ball. When you consider that the pitch of each hole in the ball may vary according to the particular whims of each bowler, you can readily see that it is possible to have an infinite number of different grips, each of which is a perfect fit.

Bowling Lane Specifications

Figure 120 indicates briefly the bowling lane specifications. The lane is 60 feet from the foul line to the 1-pin, the head pin. It is 42 inches wide and the approach is approximately 16 feet long, (12 feet from the foul line to the line marked "A"). Lanes approved by the American Bowling Congress cannot be more than forty thousandths (.040) of an inch higher or lower in any section or spot. The pins are set in a triangle, with each pin exactly 12 inches (center to center) from the pins on either side of it. ABC-sanctioned pins must weigh from 3 pounds 2 ounces to 3 pounds 10 ounces. The pin positions are numbered as in the illustration.

Lane Conditions

"Playing the lanes" is a skill acquired through years of bowling under various conditions. If the ball starts to hook sooner than usual or curves more than is nor-

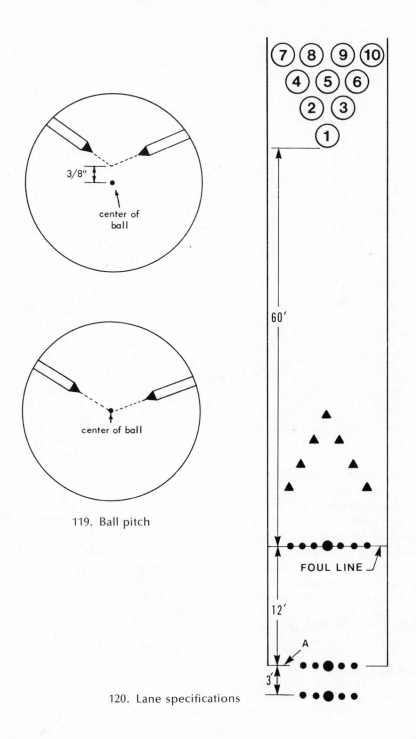

3/8"

center of
ball

center of ball

119. Ball pitch

60'

FOUL LINE

12'

A

3'

120. Lane specifications

mal, the bowler will refer to the lane as "slow" or "running." If the opposite situation is present, i.e., the ball skids farther than normal and does not take a normal break, the lane will be referred to as "fast" or "holding." Most bowlers prefer to bowl on lanes that are shaded to the slow side.

What makes a lane fast or slow? In order to answer this question you must understand how the lane is constructed and maintained. The lane is made of boards 1 to 1-1/8 inches thick and three inches wide. These boards stand on edge. From the foul line, maple boards run out the distance of sixteen feet. There they dovetail with pine boards of the same dimensions which run to within one foot of the head pin. At that point the pine boards again dovetail into maple boards, which form the pin deck, the portion of the lane on which the pins stand. A base coat of lacquer is applied to the new lane, then three or four coats of lacquer finish. When thoroughly dry, a coat of alley dressing is applied over the finish, and the lanes are ready for use. This alley dressing is nothing but a light coat of oil, which keeps the lane slightly lubricated so that the continual rolling of bowling balls does not wear through the lacquer and into the boards.

It should be obvious that if a lane is dressed too heavily with oil, or if you bowl on the lane immediately after this dressing is applied, the ball will skid further and resist the hook spin of the ball much more than if the ball were rolled on a lane that was free of oil. This dressing does not help to produce high scores if it is applied heavily to the pin deck. The ball will lose much of its traction on the lane surface and will not dig in to knock down the 5-pin on a strike hit. Also, the pin fall is not generally as effective under these conditions, because the pins tend to slide rather than to topple. The good bowler will never worry about fast or slick lane conditions at the head of the lane, as long as the last ten to twenty feet and pin deck are not oily so that the ball will dig in in this critical area.

Assuming the lanes are properly maintained, other physical conditions cause lanes to vary from one to another. All boards of one type are not identical. Some contain more pitch than others, some have a wide or open grain and thus absorb lane dressing rapidly, some have a narrow grain and resist absorbing so that the dressing will remain on top of them after it has been absorbed by other boards.

As a general rule, bowlers adjust for varying conditions in one of two ways. If the lane is slow or running, they will either move their starting location a board or two to the left, or they will move the target a board or two to the right to compensate for the additional hook. Of course, opposite adjustments are made for fast or holding lanes.

Scoring the Game of Tenpins

Although scoring in bowling seems complicated to the beginner, it is quite simple once you get used to it. Here are the symbols used in scoring:

When the first ball in any frame knocks down all pins, it is a *strike* and is marked with an *X*.

If all the pins are knocked down in two rolls, it is a *spare* and is marked with a slanted line. (The 7 is the number of pins knocked down with the first ball of the frame.)

If a *split* is left after the first roll, it is marked with a circle.

If the split is converted into a spare, it is marked with a slanted line through the circle.

If pins are left standing after two shots, it is an error or a miss, and it is marked with a horizontal line.

If a bowler fouls, his score is an *F*, which is worth zero pins. (If scored on the first ball, the bowler nevertheless gets his second shot for that frame.)

If the ball is rolled in the channel or gutter, the score is a *G*, worth zero pins.

If you get a strike, your score will be ten pins—plus what you knock down on the next two rolls as a bonus in the strike frame. If you get a spare, you will receive ten pins—plus what you knock down on the next roll as a bonus in the spare frame. Remember, the first of the two small boxes within the frame records the pins knocked down with the first ball.

Following these simple rules of scoring, it is easy to determine your score in any frame. Here are some illustrations:

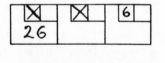

Scoring the first frame strike, remember it is worth 10 pins plus the score for the next *two* shots as a bonus.

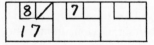

Scoring the spare made in the first frame, your score is 10 pins plus the score of the next shot as a bonus.

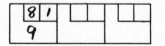

If you fail to knock down all ten pins with both rolls, your score is the total number of pins you knocked down in that frame.

Some Technical Information

Here is a sample of scoring a game or a "line":

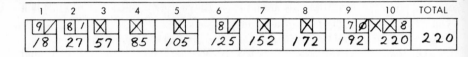

In the first frame, you knocked down all the pins with two balls, scoring a spare; show the spare symbol in the second small box. Do not record a score for the frame until after you roll your first ball in the second frame, because your score in the first frame will be ten for the spare plus what you get on the next shot as a bonus.

Your first ball in the second frame knocked down eight pins, so you add this to the ten for the spare, and you have eighteen in the first frame. Your second ball in the second frame got only one of the two standing pins, so you have an error (an open frame) and a total of nine pins for the frame. Eighteen plus nine equals twenty-seven. Your first ball in the third frame knocked down all the pins so you mark a strike in the little box, but you don't add anything until you roll two more balls. In the fourth frame, you get another strike—making it a "double"—but you still show no score; remember, a strike gives you ten, plus your next *two* balls, so you have to wait for another ball.

In the fifth frame, you get a third strike, and three in a row is called a "turkey." Now we can add up the scoring in the third frame. Ten for the strike, plus ten and ten for the next two balls, making a total of thirty pins to be added to your score in the third frame, or 27 plus 30 equals 57. This is why 12 strikes in a row makes the perfect "300" game—it is simply 30 pins per frame for 10 frames. Notice how the score mounts when you bunch the strikes! In the sixth frame, you got eight pins with the first roll. Now you can add up your score for the fourth frame—it is ten plus the next two rolls (on which you got ten and eight). This makes 28 added to the 57 in the third frame, which makes 85 in the fourth frame. The conversion of the spare in the sixth frame gives you your score for the fifth frame (10 plus 8 plus 2 added to 85 makes 105 in the fifth frame). Follow the scoring for the rest of the game.

Notice that the tenth frame is the last frame to be scored. Any roll or rolls after the tenth frame are only to compute your score in previous frames. In our example above, you got a strike on your first roll in the tenth frame. This strike gives you ten, plus two more rolls only. On the first extra roll you got 10 pins (a strike) and on the second extra roll, you got eight. This completes the game, as you do not get to roll at the two remaining pins.

How to Score a Foul. The foul line and what constitutes a foul are explained in section 2. Section 3 gives methods used for the correction of fouling. Now you must consider what the foul does to your score. When a foul is committed, the ball counts as a roll, but no pinfall is credited to your score. In other words, you treat a foul for scoring purposes the same way you would score a ball rolled in the channel—no score for that roll.

Handicaps for Scoring

As the word indicates, a handicap is an "equalizer" which enables the lower average bowler to compete with the higher average bowler. Without some type of handicap system, the higher average bowlers would win most of the time. All leagues are run on a handicap basis (with the exception of scratch leagues, which have no handicaps but must employ rigid maximum and minimum average requirements to ensure that individuals or teams are evenly matched). This is generally true of tournaments, although some are run on a classification basis, where bowlers are competing only against other bowlers with similar averages. For example, a tournament may run with A, B, C, and D Classes, where C Class would include all bowlers with averages between 160 and 169.

When organizing a handicap league, an arbitrary figure must be selected from which to figure the handicaps. The figure generally selected is 200, though it may be higher or lower. The figure selected is called the *scratch figure* for that league. A percentage of the difference between the bowler's average and the scratch figure is then allowed as handicap. The percentage generally used is two-thirds. For example:

Scratch figure	200	
Bowler's average	179	
Difference	21	
Per game handicap	14	(if using 2/3 as the basis of handicap)

Each bowler's handicap is figured in a similar manner and is added to his total pins to determine his score for each game. The American Bowling Congress and the Women's International Bowling Congress (A.B.C and W.I.B.C.) provide handicap charts at no charge. When figuring handicaps or averages, always drop any fractions. If the handicap figures to be 24-3/4, use 24 per game.

14. GLOSSARY OF BOWLING TERMS AND SLANG

A.B.C. The American Bowling Congress.

A.J.B.C. The American Junior Bowling Congress.

Alley The lane.

Approach The area on which the bowler takes his steps to the foul line; also the act of moving to the foul line to deliver the ball.

Anchor man The fifth or last man in the team line-up. Usually the best bowler.

Baby-split The 2–7 or the 3–10 split.

Back-up A ball that fades to the right (for a right-hander) on its way down the lane.

Barmaid Any pin "hidden" directly behind another; also called a "sleeper."

Bedposts The 7–10 split; also called "goalposts."

Big fill A good count on the first roll following a spare–eight or nine pins.

Big four The 4–6–7–10 split; also called "double pinochle."

Blind score An absent bowler's score.

Blow An error.

Bridge The edge-to-edge distance between the finger holes.

Brooklyn Hitting the left side of the head pin (for a right-hander).

Bucket The 2–4–5–8 spare leave for a right-hander.

Cheesecake A lane that is very easy to score on; also called a "pie alley," or a "soft alley."

Cherry Chopping off the front pin or pins on a spare shot.

Choke To tighten up under pressure.

Count The number of pins knocked down with the first ball.

Dead ball A poorly rolled ball, one that deflects or bounces excessively.

Division boards Where the maple boards and pine boards dovetail into one another about 16 feet from the foul line; also called the splice.

Dodo ball A term used in the old days for an illegal (weighted) ball.

Double Two strikes in succession.

Dutchman A 200 game made by alternating strikes and spares.

Error A missed spare; same as a blow.

Flat apple or **flat ball** Same as a dead ball.

Foul Touching anywhere beyond the foul line.

Foul line The black line separating the lane and the approach.

Foundation   Also a "good foundation," meaning a strike in the ninth frame.

Frame   One of the ten frames in a game; also a box.

Goalposts   The 7–10 split.

Graveyard   The toughest lanes on which to produce good scores.

Groove   Supposedly a "trough" in a lane all the way to the pocket, thereby making scoring much easier.

Gutter   The troughs on either side of the lane; also called channels.

Handicap   As the name indicates, an adjustment in scores to compensate for unequal matching.

Head pin   The number one pin; the front pin.

Holding alley   Same as a fast alley; one that cuts down on the amount of hook.

Jersey hit   Same as a Brooklyn hit.

Kegler   A bowler.

Kickbacks   The sideboards at the pit end of the lanes.

Kingpin   The five pin.

Leadoff   The first man in the line-up.

Lofting   Throwing the ball onto the lane from a position that is too upright thereby causing the ball to thump as it hits the lane.

Mark   Getting either a strike or a spare.

Nose hit   Hitting the head pin dead center on the first ball.

Open frame   A frame with neither a strike nor spare.

P.B.A.   Professional Bowlers Association.

Picket fence   The 1–2–4–7 or the 1–3–6–10 leave.

Pie alley   A "soft" alley; one on which it is easy to score.

Pitch   The angle at which holes are bored into bowling balls.

Pocket   The space between the 1–3 pins for right-handers; the space between the 1–2 pins for left-handers.

Powerhouse   A very strong hooking ball that seems to tear the pins apart.

Pumpkin   The opposite of a powerhouse; a very weak ball.

Railroad   A split leave, such as the 8–10, the 7–10, the 4–6, or the 7–9.

Return   The track on which the ball rolls back to the bowler from the pit.

Running lane   A slow lane that allows more hook.

Runway   The approach area.

Scratch   Actual scores without handicap.

Sleeper   A barmaid; a hidden pin in a leave.

Soft alley   A lane that is easy to score on; a pie alley.

Spare   The score for knocking down all the pins with the two balls of a single frame.

Split   Two or more nonadjacent pins left standing after the first roll, neither of which is the head pin.

Squash   A dead or lifeless ball.

Stiff alley   A "fast" or "holding" alley; one that resists the ball's tendency to hook.

Strike   The score for knocking down all the pins with the first ball of a frame.

Strike out   To roll three strikes in the tenth frame.

Sweeper   A hook ball that works well and "sweeps" the pins off the lane into the pit.

Tap   A pin left standing after an apparently good strike hit.

Thin hit   A "light" hit; one that does not have enough "pocket."

Three points   Rolling the ball between the pins left in a split, missing both of them; a reference to a football field goal score.

Turkey   Three successive strikes by one bowler in a single game.

Washout   The 1–2–4–10 leave for a right-hander; the 1–3–6–7 leave for a left-hander.

W.I.B.C.   Women's International Bowling Congress.

Working ball   A very effective ball having a lot of hook spin.

Y.B.A.   Youth Bowling Association.